I0127233

The Worlds
Educators Create

For my wife, Krysten
You are my center point in such a vast and confusing world

Contents

Foreword

Madison West high school has an innocuous two-door exit on the northeast corner of the three-story building. The idea, I think, was to provide a necessary emergency point of egress—in an emergency, 2,000 students and faculty shouldn't be bottlenecking at the main multi-door entrances on Ash Street to the east or Regent Street to the south. But it seems clear the northeast-corner exit was not designed for regular use. In order to use it as an entrance, one has to scramble up a stone retaining wall to the side lawn that approaches the door or else climb a flight of exterior stairs to reach the same point. And, obviously, using it as an exit requires bounding down the bouldery retaining wall or the stairs. The building's designers sited several other doors on the ground floor, opening right onto the level of Van Hise Avenue on the building's north side. Planting a two-door exit at the building's northeast corner was an architectural afterthought, a mere and almost formal nod to fire-code necessity.

And yet at lunchtime, that little exit was constantly packed. When I attended the school, almost 30 years ago, the administration had set up three staggered lunch periods of only 35 minutes each. The school had an open campus policy, which students were eager to use, and I suspect that the short lunch periods were designed to keep students from straying too far or from getting into too much trouble. If you had a fourth-period class on the northeast side of the school, on any of the three floors, then that little exit was your best bet to maximize your freedom—when the bell rang, the hallways filled immediately to capacity, and it would take longer to make one's way to a larger exit than it would to take advantage of the northeast stairwell to reach that little two-door egress to the outside.

My two best friends shared my lunch period for most of our years there, and one of them lived only a couple blocks from school, right off of Van Hise Avenue. So that little exit on the northeast corner of the building was where we'd meet, only seconds, it seemed, after the bell dismissed us from fourth period. We had our lunchtime routine fully dialed in. Three minutes to reach his house; only a couple more minutes to get individual pots of water boiling for ramen; and enough remaining time to watch an entire 22-minute episode of _The Simpsons_ that he'd taped at some point on VHS, all before we hustled back to school for fifth period.

I had never once thought about the central role that the little northeast-corner exit played in some of the most important informal learning and social-development experiences of my high school life—nor about all the accidents of architectural design and school policy that made it the affordance that it was—until I read this magnificent and eye-opening work by Matt Clay.

As he very correctly points out, and as has certainly been my experience as both student and teacher, schooling tends to conspire to suppress the particularities of place, to filter them out. Sitting in my third-floor English classroom during my junior year, staring out the window (but really listening, Mr. Lyon, I promise!), I knew, obviously, that I was looking out at the tops of the trees sloping down through residential neighborhoods and past the agriculture school and all the way to Lake Mendota. But I also knew that Aristotle's unities of time, place, and action—which Mr. Lyon was explaining to us, and to which I was definitely listening—were, somewhat ironically, supposed to be timeless and placeless.

It did not matter to my learning that the land flowed the way that it did outside the window; it was not relevant that the university marching band's practice was audible early in the school year when the weather was still warm enough to keep the windows open. The nip in the air as October rolled around, or the serious bite of the first week back from winter break—these were not _telling_ us anything, as far as school was concerned; they were not educationally relevant. The irony of the fact that I still remember some of the opening lines from Act II of _As You Like It_, which I memorized for Mr. Lyon's class—"as the icy fang / And churlish chiding of the winter's wind, / Which when it bites and blows upon my body / Even till I shrink with cold, I smile and say / 'This is no flattery. These are counselors / That feelingly persuade me what I am'"—is not lost on me. The actual icy fang of an actual winter's wind? Not important. Shakespeare's praise of its ability to feelingly persuade me what I am? Now, that's important.

I think my school was fairly typical of a tendency that Matt diagnoses in this book: More even than failing to _attend_ to place, or to orient students to place, schooling has actually striven to shut the particularities of place out of the schoolhouse entirely, the better, perhaps, to connect students to what we might call the curriculum most general, the curriculum as abstract. And then, awkwardly, from within this framework, teachers are asked to work conscientiously—and, all too often, idiosyncratically—to make that most general curriculum "relevant" to students' lives. The first move pretends that students exist nowhere in particular. The second move tries to meet them where they are.

The Worlds Educators Create does not ask teachers to suture this paradox by adding token references to geographical features or activities pertaining to local environmental issues. This book is after something equally practical but far more ambitious: a fundamental reorientation of the educational endeavor such that the paradox itself simply dissolves. Locating "place" at the center of the educational experience facilitates a grounded approach to what I earlier called the curriculum most general, but it also makes the educational tasks of envisioning and realizing justice, mutuality, and care part of a seamless whole rather than a patchwork of occasionally contradictory impulses and methods. It is likely the case that educational institutions at the district, state, and federal level will need to change in order to fully achieve what Clay sketches here. But that does not mean that those institutions must take the lead. Clay's book is aimed at classroom teachers precisely because the necessary transformations lie perennially within their grasp. Clay does not ask teachers to do *more*. He simply asks them to do *differently*.

Derek Gottlieb, associate professor of teacher education
at the University of Northern Colorado

Preface

Hindsight provides an interesting opportunity to see how series of seemingly random choices lead to moments of profound impact for our lives. One of these moments for me was during my first summer as a doctoral student at the University of Northern Colorado. It was during that summer that I clearly remember sitting on the tailgate of my pickup at night at an overlook in Rocky Mountain National Park doing homework by the glow of my laptop screen. However, I struggled to focus on my work as I watched the line of headlights stream out of the park because all I could think was, "We are getting something in education profoundly wrong."

The series of decisions that led to that moment, choosing a blended doctoral program so I could continue teaching high school full time in Western Kansas and then choosing to save money on the trip out for classes by tent camping near the national park, seem inconsequential compared to the weight of that moment. I grew up spending a lot of time outdoors and at that particular moment I was sitting looking at a landscape which meant so much to me it would be the inspiration for my sons' middle names. However, the line of people leaving looked no more engaged with the place than a drive to the grocery store.

Whether the occupants of those particular cars I watched have or have not connected to that particular national park, I have no actual idea. However, they have served as a constant visual reminder that as the education profession we have struggled to engage many students in and for place. There have been many possible advocates for place go through classrooms, national parks, and countless other educational settings without the opportunity being seized.

My feeling in that moment and in much of my career since is that the failure to engage students with place is not an intentional action but really one that arises from not having the curricular and pedagogical tools necessary. These are opportunities missed without most educators realizing the opportunity ever existed at all. In short, I feel that we have lacked the language and frameworks necessary to be able to identify what we are at risk of losing. The aim of this book is to provide that language and frameworks.

Many books claim grand new visions to completely reimagine education, but that is not my goal. I believe much of what takes place in educational settings works incredibly well and is impactful. However, we have had limited tools to be able to define "working" in all but the narrowest sense. As someone who believes firmly in the value of place, my aim is to provide lenses that we can use to look at educational practice to determine if it is working with regards to its impact on communities and landscapes.

For the reader of this book, I first want to thank you for at least being open to the possibility of engaging in this work. There are virtually limitless issues competing for the attention of educators, and as someone who cares deeply about place, I greatly appreciate that you have chosen to invest your limited time toward this one. Second, I want to clarify that I do not believe there is one correct way to teach for and about place. Your individualities as an educator and your particular setting require a high degree of personalization. As such this book is focused on how to think about place, not what to think about place.

My goal instead is to give you tools as an educator to look at your own practice, curricula, and/or policies to consider the impact of each on the creation of place. I do not believe that most educators make wrong decisions related to their practice and place but instead do not realize they are making a decision at all. In this book, it is my hope that you will see the decisions you are making as an educator and that moving forward you will make purposeful decisions that reflect your values, perspectives, and interests as an educator.

Acknowledgments

This book is in no small way the direct and indirect result of the many great educators, friends, family, and colleagues that have invested in me over my life and career. I am eternally for all of those who have taken the extra time to investment in me as an individual, challenge my thinking, and push me to continue to grow. Those individuals and experiences have made me who I am today.

I would like to particularly recognize the many great colleagues who have challenged and encouraged me, especially those from the American Association for Teaching and Curriculum and the Kansas Association for Conservation and Environmental Education. There is tremendous power in finding a professional home among positive peers and I am so grateful that I have found two.

I would also like to recognize the amazing coworkers and colleagues I have at Fort Hays State University. On a daily basis I am reminded of how fortunate I am to work such caring and supportive individuals. In particular, I would like to thank my department chair, Chris Jochum, for encouraging me to pursue this project, answering countless questions, and connecting with the wonderful folks at Rowman & Littlefield.

Growing up as a small-town Kansas kid, I am incredibly grateful to have happened upon Derek Gottlieb and I am eternally grateful for his mentorship. His patience in dealing with my tendency to have scholarly eyes larger than my metaphorical stomach is truly staggering. As a truly great mentor he has helped me discover my strengths and become a version of my academic self of which I am truly proud.

Most of all, I would like to thank my family. My parents Ken and Donnel Clay have always believed in and challenged me. I would also like to thank my wife, Krysten, and my three sons, Malachi, Merrick, and Macklin. Their daily lives have been the most impacted by my work on this book as I write, edit, and struggle to condense ideas into cohesive paragraphs. Most admirably, they took on this role without blinking.

Finally, I would be remiss in a book about place to not recognize the two landscapes which have most shaped who I am: Rocky Mountain National Park and the High Plains of Western Kansas. Not only have these served as the physical setting for much of my reflection in writing this book, they have served as the litmus test for comparing my ideas to actual physical places.

Introduction

Now more than ever, educators are asked to take on increasingly difficult and diverse roles. Especially in light of the drastic interruption of the Covid-19 pandemic, it has become increasingly clear the range of roles educators play in communities. Unfortunately, these increasing roles for educators have not necessarily come with increased time or resources. In many ways, educators are asked to perform a "loaves and fishes"-type miracle every single day.

In exploring the relationship between education and place, this book is not seeking to add another responsibility on educators' plates. Rather, the opportunity here is to recognize the connection that already exists and think differently about how educators can approach their work in curriculum design, instructional planning, and assessment. The goal is to provide a new lens educators can apply to their work.

To truly explore the link between place and education, it is important to both conceptualize and contextualize place. In conceptualizing place, the goal is to dive into considering what place means, and more importantly what it means for teaching. It is also critical to explore who individuals are as educators to consider how that impacts their perceptions of and interactions with place. However, most importantly educators must consider how the treatment of place in education shapes individual communities as well as society as a whole.

In contextualizing place, the goal is to translate the larger conceptual understanding of place into educational practice. Although this can take the form of classroom lessons or activities, these practices might also apply at the curriculum level or in informal educational settings. Additionally, there are the opportunities to consider the messages communicated about place beyond the intended curriculum, such as through the exclusion of particular perspectives or contexts of place.

GUIDING QUESTIONS

This exploration of place will be shaped by five guiding questions. Although the answers for these questions certainly vary between individuals and more than likely the responses will continue to evolve over time, they are critical to ensuring that education contributes toward development and creation of place. The aim is not for each educator to answer these questions definitively, but rather to continue to revisit and reflect on these both in our understanding and our practice.

1. *What is place?*

   To consider what place is, it is important to start without an expectation of arriving at a single, neat definition. Place is a plurality existing on multiple levels at the same time.[1] Moreover, what place *is* and what place *means* can be very different, even for a single individual. Trying to condense all of these meanings into a single definition or explanation would ultimately exclude some meanings. In terms of mindset, instead of searching for a single definition, the goal is to look at diverse ideas, perspectives, and experiences to answer "which are place?"

2. *How does place factor into teaching?*

   During the era of standardization in education, it would be entirely possible for educators to go day to day in their work without giving much, if any, consideration to the role of place. However, teaching and learning always occur in physical spaces. Teachers teach in actual classrooms, in real communities. Even during distance learning, students learn in tangible locations, even if those places are not the same as the teacher and/or are in front of computer screens in their homes. In recognizing that teaching and learning always exist in a place, the question is not "Does place factor into teaching?," but how.

3. *How can teaching practices be analyzed for place?*

   In building on the question of how place factors into teaching, it is also important to explore tools for analyze the impacts of particular educational practices and curricula. These tools are especially important in looking at lessons or activities that may not explicitly aim to teach about place, but which will carry implicit messages about perspectives and value of place. Additionally, the tools will be critical in evaluating current teaching practices and curricula for treatment of place to consider how they can be adapted, rather than assuming that teaching for the improvement of place requires a complete redesign of educational practices.

4. *How can instruction be designed for place?*

Although there are certainly opportunities to adapt existing teaching practices and lessons, teaching for the improvement and expansion of place invites educators to design instruction toward that particular aim. The goal in designing this instruction is not only to focus on incorporating the local place, but also to look for the inclusion of place beyond the local as a way to provide richer meaning to content. The complexity of place also provides an opportunity and need from cross-curricular instructional design to truly allow students to explore multiple facets of place.

5. *How does education for place inspire action?*

The final, and most critical, question to explore requires that educators recognize that in teaching for the expansion of place, the aims cannot be knowledge alone, but action. The educational outcomes that will lead to an advancement of place are not those that can be easily measured through a test or worksheet; rather, these outcomes require that students engage in and with place, both local and distant. Ultimately, these aims require educators to think more broadly in how they design instruction and assess learning to consider their work for the role it plays in the creation of place.

STRUCTURE OF CHAPTERS

In the chapters ahead, you will explore place from both conceptual and contextual perspectives. Although these chapters will introduce a range of perspectives and examples, ultimately determining how place impacts teaching practice is a very individual process. To help in this journey there will be reflection questions at the end of each chapter. Consider not only reflecting on these questions, but recording your responses somewhere that you can revisit them. As educators, understanding one's own journey in understanding and connecting to place can be a critical tool in helping to guide students.

NOTES

1. Soja, Edward. *Thirdspace: Journeys to Los Angeles and Other Real and Imagined Places*. Hoboken, NJ: Blackwell, 1996.

Chapter 1

Work Worth Doing

There are countless pressures and stressors vying for the attention of educators when it comes to improving practice. Among calls to be more attentive to the needs of diverse learners, reflect on how to create relevance in curricula, and to extend learning beyond the school day, there is a fascinating question that has been largely under-explored: What is the relationship between education and place?

As the educational theorist Arne Naess suggested, "I'm not much interested in ethics or morals. I'm interested in how we experience the world."[1] The opportunity to consider the role educators have in the creation, preservation, and expansion of place is a vast landscape with few roads but many beautiful sites to explore. Moreover, it is a landscape in which teachers can more fully recognize and communicate the impact of their work, as well as find opportunities for artistic expression.

The lack of attention given to exploring the relationship between place and education is not for lack of opportunity. All education, formal or informal, urban, rural, or otherwise, occurs in a place. Specific to the types of places labeled as nature or wilderness, the potential audience is abundant. In 2021, nearly 300 million visitors entered national parks in the United States.[2] In the same year, over half of Americans over the age of six participated in outdoor recreation of some kind.[3]

These massive potential audiences exist, at least partially, in addition to the over 50 million public school students in the United States.[4] In short, the potential to engage learners in exploring and connecting with places both near and distant is plentiful. However, this is an opportunity which many educators allow to slip past while focused on other, seemingly more pressing goals.

With the ever-expanding litany of environmental crises, the need for educational practices that inspire students, traditional or otherwise, to take action could not be more evident. The millions of individuals and students who enter national parks, nature areas, and classrooms every year serve as an opportunity that is largely missed. As the time remaining to protect places from impending threat of climate change ticks steadily away, it is critical for educators to take a purposeful and intentional role in inspiring students to engage with place.

The overlapping domains of environmental education, place-based education, and science education can make for a confusing landscape to say the least. There are concepts, ideologies, and practices that cross between the three, and others that are uniquely categorized in just one focus. Even more challenging, this murkiness exists against the backdrop of all of the other pressures placed on educators, such as standardized testing, responding to individual student needs, and, in the past few years, teaching through a global pandemic.

In many cases this leaves teachers asked to implement strategies without having been given the opportunity to really explore the big-picture aims of those strategies. The goal of this book is to provide space for thinking about those big-picture aims, while also translating those ideas into educational practices. In other words, this is an opportunity for teachers to consider their practice not just in terms of particular academic outcomes, but by what it means for their community as a whole.

In starting an exploration of the connection between place and education, it is critical to first recognize that places are not objective or fixed. Henri Lefebvre argued, "Every social space is the outcome of a process with many aspects and many contributing currents, signifying and nonsignifying, perceived and directly experienced, practical and theoretical."[5] This means that place is not just the setting in which teaching occurs, but the product of a number of factors including education itself.

Education does not just lead to how much students know about place, but actually influences what the place *is*. As a result, instead of treating place as content in education, the goal is to explore place, at least partially, as an *outcome* of education. More fairly, since place is constantly changing it is not really a product of education, but more a project of education. It is really a dependent in need of constant care and attention.

INTENTIONALITY

The critical shift in perspective to viewing place as an outcome of education instead of just content, or worse yet—superfluous to the work of education— is that it means that participation is not optional for educators. By the nature of their role in their communities, educators will teach something about the places in which they work. However, in many cases what is taught is left as an afterthought. The messages about place became a happenstance of curricula.

Rather than passively letting these lessons occur, there is an opportunity for educators to be intentional in what they teach about place.

In all likelihood, the greatest challenge to creating meaningful experiences and teaching impactful lessons related to place is not educators that think through all of the elements and make the "wrong" decision, but educators who do not realize they are making a decision at all. The call here is not for educators to start teaching about place; by virtue of their role they are already doing that. Instead, the aim is for educators to be intentional in what and how they teach about place.

WORK WORTH DOING

In facing the daunting task of exploring both what place means for education, and more importantly the role educators have in the creation and expansion of place, it could be tempting to wish for the apparently easier option of just focusing directly on specific content. When placed in the current turbulent times in education it becomes even easier to put this in the category of "maybe when things slow down . . ." Although those options might seem easier to educators as individuals, they are in no way easier for society as a whole in the long run.

Long-term success as a society requires that educators prepare students to not only understand complex problems, but also to take initiative to solve them. It also requires that educators equip students to work to create places that are homes for equity and justice. Over the long scales of time, what is "easier" is to prepare students to face challenges head on, instead of working to mitigate these problems around the periphery.

Theodore Roosevelt suggested, "Far and away the best prize that life offers is the chance to work hard at work worth doing . . ."[6] It is not difficult to argue that preparing students to face the environmental, social, and political challenges of the present and future falls well within the category of "work worth doing." As you move forward to really dig into the role education has in the creation and expansion of place, consider this an invitation to really dig into this work worth doing.

REFLECTION QUESTIONS

1. In what ways is place present already in your teaching practice and might this provide an opportunity for a starting point?
2. What experiences have you had with place as a learner? What do you remember about these experiences and how they impacted you?

3. What elements or characteristics of your current place are you most
eager to emphasize or integrate into your teaching practice?

NOTES

1. Warwick Fox, *Toward a Transpersonal Ecology: Developing New Foundations for Environmentalism* (Albany, NY: State University of New York Press, 1995).

2. National Park Service, "NPS Visitation 2021," National Parks Service (U.S. Department of the Interior), accessed October 25, 2022, https://www.nps.gov/orgs /1207/most-famous-national-parks-set-visitation-records-in-2021.htm.

3. Outdoor Industry Association, "Outdoor Participation Report 2015," accessed October 25, 2022, https://outdoorindustry.org/wp-content/uploads/2016/07/ ResearchParticipation2015.pdf.

4. Maya Riser-Kositsky, "Education Statistics: Facts about American Schools," *Education Week*, August 2, 2022, https://www.edweek.org/leadership/education -statistics-facts-about-american-schools/2019/01.

5. Henri Lefebvre, *The Production of Space*, trans. Donald Nicholson-Smith (Malden, MA: Blackwell, 2009), 110.

6. Theodore Roosevelt, "Address to the New York State Agricultural Association, Syracuse, NY," September 7, 1903. The American Presidency Project. https://www .presidency.ucsb.edu/documents/address-the-new-york-state-agricultural-association -syracuse-ny.

Chapter 2

The Role of Place in Education

To dive into the role of place in education, it is first critical to explore what education about, or for, place really means. At its simplest, education about place is the communication of messages, ideas, values, perspectives, or concepts of the place. Education about place includes both the intentional and unintentional messages communicated about place. Additionally, education about place occurs in a number of different settings.

In this broad definition, education about place includes teaching in formal educational settings such as K-12 classrooms, interpretation or instruction in informal educational settings such as zoos and nature settings, and communication about place through media such as books, curricula, or videos. Essentially, to teach about place one is transmitting a message about place, or facilitating the development of a perspective about place, to another. Although this definition of teaching about place is simple, when considering the depth of place, the practice takes on complexity.

In order to truly consider how deep of a concept place is, and by extension the perspectives that have been applied to teaching it, it is perhaps best to compare a place to a painting of a landscape. The painting includes many colors and is incredibly detailed. In fact, the level of detail is such that it is impossible for the viewer to take in the entire painting at once. As a result, it is best for the viewer to use a set of colored-lens glasses.

Each pair of glasses holds lenses that are a different color and each pair blocks some aspects of the painting, but allows others to remain visible. Each of these pair of glasses represent the lenses discussed in the coming pages. They come from a variety of academic disciplines and each reveal and conceal certain aspects of the painting. Ultimately, some academic disciplines combine multiple of these lenses. However, the essential point is that no single lens or even pair of lenses can truly reveal the entire painting.

In exploring these lenses, the goal is not to give a detailed, itemized history of how place has been taught. Rather, the aim is to understand all of the angles of education that fall under the large umbrella of place. Consider this as more of identifying landmarks within the broad scope of the topic of place, rather than setting boundaries. It is also critical to remember that each of these perspectives carry messages about place, even if they are not explicit.

David Orr wrote, "All education is environmental education."[1] In this argument he was making the case that all teaching carried messaged about environmental values, or lack thereof. Similarly, all teaching carries a message about place, whether intentional or unintentional, through inclusion or omission. That is to say, not teaching about place is not an option. Rather, opting out is electing to only teach about place passively.

LENSES OF PLACE

The lenses discussed here borrow from an approach utilized in earth systems science.[2] However, the lenses typically used in earth systems science are far from encompassing all of the perspectives that have been used to teach about place. Each of the lenses is really a component or subsystem of place and is described here as a sphere. Spheres typically included in this approach are the biosphere, hydrosphere, atmosphere, and lithosphere or geosphere. Occasionally the cryosphere is also considered among this group.

This set represents a wide range of natural science disciplines. However, to have the necessary lenses to more fully glimpse place, it is important to consider the anthroposphere, chronosphere, and pneumatosphere. Again, each of these spheres do not necessarily represent new or novel approaches toward viewing or teaching place, but it is critical to recognize how each can contribute toward a clearer vision of place as a whole. It is also worth noting that a number of instructional and inquiry approaches exist which bridge or combine these spheres, including such fields as ecology or environmental justice.

These are great examples of the need to combine multiple lenses to truly understand a place. In dealing with each of these spheres separately, the intention is not to ignore contributions of the many important angles of instruction and inquiry which are interdisciplinary. Rather, the aim is to clarify the different lenses that do exist, before considering the revelations that might come from combining them.

The biosphere represents the living things of a place. Historically, teaching about the biosphere was organized into disciplines such as zoology or botany. In most primary and secondary schools this now falls under the category of life science or biology. In approaching place, these content areas tend to address what lives "there." However, there can be a wide range in how "there" is defined. There are courses and curricula that focus on very specific geographic areas, such as regional natural history courses, and seek to make students familiar with the specific lifeforms that occupy their immediate surroundings.

However, as curricula become increasingly standardized, "there" can come to constitute the entire planet. As a result, representative or generic life forms are included in these lessons. This can take the form of focusing on the large mammals of the African veldt, or inserting generic birds or snakes into books or worksheets. To whatever degree of specificity, ultimately the biosphere lens prepares students to view place in terms of what lives there.

In approaching studying place, the hydrosphere lens looks at water within the place. The hydrosphere might appear in courses that deal with topics as the water cycle in earth science or the geographic distribution of oceans, lakes, rivers, and streams. However, it is important to recognize the very dramatic role water places in shaping the distribution of people on a landscape.

Especially in arid and semiarid regions such as the American west, water is central in planning human and economic developmentally, as Wallace Stegner highlighted in his biography of John Wesley Powell.[3] There is a reason water is often compared to the lifeblood of a landscape, as the health and survival of the creatures that live there, both human and nonhuman, are bound to the availability of water. Moreover, watersheds represent a key aspect in which places blend together. Jackson Hole, Wyoming and Sioux City, Iowa are very different communities, but the actions of both will ultimately impact the Missouri River.

Closely related to the hydrosphere, and crossing into many of the same disciplines, is the cryosphere, which consists of the frozen water on earth, including glaciers, ice caps, ice sheets, and snow pack. Although these impacts are obviously most dramatic in particular geographic areas, such as highly glaciated areas such as the Norwegian fjords, it is critical to remember that the impacts of the cryosphere can be experienced far from the snow and ice itself. Specifically, the impacts of rising sea levels due to melting ice sheets and downstream drought from decreasing snow pack can be very relevant and prominent.

The atmosphere describes the gases which surround the earth. This is a topic that often appears in earth science courses, but also includes the two other directly connected disciplines of meteorology and climatology. Weather, when thought of simply, is the condition of the atmosphere for an area. Although weather is often included as a topic in classrooms at the elementary and secondary level, it is also included in many more aspects of education.

Physical settings and designs of schools often reflect the weather of the area, from the open campus designs in southern Arizona to enclosed walkways of schools in the high mountain communities of Colorado. Weather is also a topic that carries over into policies such as dress codes, approaches to recesses, and activities available to students. Similarly, climate, and in particular the impacts of climate change, are noticeably impactful on schools. Increases in extreme weather events such as large winter storms, wildfire, and hurricanes have impacted school schedules or in some cases forced schools to close for periods of time.

The final sphere focused primarily within traditional scientific disciplines is the lithosphere. The lithosphere, sometimes referred to as the geosphere, represents the solid material of earth's crust including rocks, soil, mountains, canyons, and other physical geologic formations. Beyond obvious inclusion in earth science classes, the lithosphere also has a dramatic impact on careers available in an area, and as a result, career-focused education.

How and where agriculture, mining, and oil and gas extraction occur is dependent on characteristics of the lithosphere. Additionally, the lithosphere determines the risks posed to a particular area through hazards such as flooding or earthquakes. Although these five spheres, especially when combined, provide a wide lens as to the nature and characteristics of place, there are still shortcomings as well as areas in which place is encountered in schools.

A critical point in recognizing areas outside of the natural science disciplines where place is taught in schools is to consider that places, as we experience them, are really just a single frame within an extremely long film. The history of place in the case of human history for most places goes back thousands of years and in geologic terms typically millions. Labeled as a sphere, this can be thought of as the chronosphere to represent the passage of time. Within schools this often is included in history courses and lessons.

What and who is included in teaching the history of place can be extremely powerful in shaping students' understanding of place. Additionally, this lens to consider place through the passage of time is important in allowing students to understand place as something undergoing constant change, rather than a fixed entity. In short, this lens allows students to come to see that they are not the only ones to have experienced a place.

Considering the human experience in place falls within the anthroposphere, or the sum total of human presence within a place. Although this might seem like a topic that in schools would fall within a narrow band of social and natural science courses, the reality is that this is a perspective also very prominent within courses and programs focused on career and technical education. The types of careers available to students and the focal areas in career and technical education rely heavily on the characteristics of the place, and also communicate messages about the place for students.

For example, programs focused on preparation for careers in industries such as agriculture, mining, and oil and gas prepare students to view a place for what resources can be extracted from it, but a focus on tourism and hospitality could lead students to see the need to preserve or conserve a place to encourage more visitors. Similarly, technology courses and instruction will impact how students understand their presence in place. Although technology can allow for a much deeper understanding of place through increased access to information, an emphasis that place does not have a role in a technologically rich society might lead students to students having a reduced sense of place.

The final lens to consider here is one that is likely not in the formal curriculum of most schools in the United States, especially public schools. However, it is critical to consider because it is one many students will use in making sense of place, which will be referenced here as the pneumatosphere, or the total of human spirituality. Whereas the other seven lenses carry an element of objectivity or verifiability, albeit impacted by perception, the pneumatosphere consists of interpretations which may not rely only on observable qualities.

Similarly, the pneumatosphere might ascribe values and meaning to a place that might extend beyond those which arise from more objective observable characteristics alone. Although it is easiest to imagine this lens applied to overtly religious sites such as Mecca, the Western Wall, or the Ganges River, it can also be applied to understanding places that may not be thought of as traditionally religious.

For example, the lithosphere lens would use geologic evidence to interpret the Grand Canyon and Devils Tower to be the results of geologic processes based on observable characteristics of the rock. However, religious perspectives might interpret these to be the result of a great flood or a giant bear, respectively.[45] A spiritual lens is used beyond just understanding how a place came to be; it can also be used in ascribing value to a place.

Whereas the biosphere, cryosphere, and lithosphere lenses might be able to highlight the value of the geologic formations, alpine organisms, and glaciers of the high Himalaya, it customary for the Sherpa people to view these places as the home of the gods, a value that would certainly exceed just being the land of some interesting rock formations.[6] Undoubtedly, spirituality is a tool which people can and do use in ascribing meaning to a place.

As an educator, the opportunity is not to memorize that all of the lenses that exist, nor certainly to try to incorporate all of them into each discussion of place within a classroom. Rather, the critical realization is to resist the isolating effect separate content areas have on the way students are, or are not, invited to experience place. Place is not a subtopic relegated to just geography or science courses. Nor is it a distraction from typical focal points in schools such as literacy and mathematics. The critical point to recognize is that place provides context for teaching, and in so doing greater meaning and value.

REFLECTION QUESTIONS

1. Which lenses do you tend to privilege in your teaching practice?
2. Which lenses might you tend to ignore and how can you better allow for students to use those to engage with place?
3. What opportunities for collaboration between content areas and individuals might arise from a more inclusive consideration of lenses of place?

NOTES

1. David W. Orr, 1992. *Ecological Literacy: Education and the Transition to a Postmodern World*. Albany, NY. State University of New York Press.

2. "How Are the Earth's Natural Systems Connected?," Florida Museum, June 17, 2020, https://www.floridamuseum.ufl.edu/earth-systems/how-are-the-earths-natural -systems-connected/.

3. Wallace Stegner, *Beyond the Hundredth Meridian: John Wesley Powell and the Second Opening of the West.* Boston: Houghton, Mifflin, 1954.

4. Yale Divinity School, "The Flood Session 4," accessed October 25, 2022, https: //divinity.yale.edu/sites/default/files/the_flood.pdf.

5. Hannah Trim, "Devils Tower—Climbing on Sacred Land," Indigenous Religious Traditions, December 18, 2011, https://sites.coloradocollege.edu/indigenoustraditions /sacred-lands/devils-tower-climbing-on-sacred-land/.

6. Johan Reinhard, "The Sacred Himalaya," AAC Publications—The Sacred Himalaya, accessed October 25, 2022, http://publications.americanalpineclub.org/articles /12198712300/The-Sacred-Himalaya.

Chapter 3

Expansive Place and the Crisis of Connectedness

As someone who grew up with numerous family experiences in the outdoors and camping, it is odd that I have a key memory related to doing dishes at a campsite. However, a particular chore doing moment from my first time taking high school students to the Rocky Mountains has firmly etched itself in my brain as an educator. In that moment it became abundantly clear to me how privileged I am to have grown up with experiences in nature.

After a particularly difficult day of hiking, and an evening meal, I grabbed a headlamp and the couple dishes to walk down the hill in the campground to the dishwashing station. As I started to walk down the hill I heard a student call out after me.

"Can I come with you?"

"Sure," I replied, "But I am just going to do dishes . . . " I trailed off a bit assuming the student must have assumed I was doing something considerably more fun, but he seemed undeterred by the apparently monotonous task. We chatted about the hike from the day and what we had seen. The student tried to hide the little grimace of pain with each step as he walked on legs quite sore from traveling on foot in the mountainous terrain. Among the small talk, he rather abruptly blurted out something rather profound.

"I didn't know I loved being in places like this until I was here. This isn't something my family does, but I think we could. I think my brothers would like it." He then carried on about the beauty and wildness of the landscape and how he felt while exploring a new place. The sudden change from being in the outdoors as something he saw that he did not do, to very suddenly something he can do and, more importantly, enjoy really hit me. He was immensely capable of encountering and interpreting a place, but did not realize so until given the opportunity.

To truly understand the need for a new framework in approaching the connection between place and education, it is first important to understand the limitations of existing approaches, perspectives, and lenses. Essentially, the task is to understand the limitations of these approaches and, more importantly, how they may be falling short of the ultimate aims in teaching about place. However, this first requires clarifying what these ultimate aims are.

AIMS AND OUTCOMES IN TEACHING OF PLACE

In many subsets of education, across content areas, student ages, and educational settings, aims tend to be conceived of only in terms of content to be transmitted. From this perspective, an impactful educator for place would be one that successfully allows all of their students to come to know something about a place, perhaps details of the history, culture, flora, or fauna. In identifying these particular outcomes, it is easy to analyze the impacts of particular teaching strategies. Although often the outcomes that are officially described in curricula, realistically these are not the outcomes which most educators of place truly wish to inspire in their students.

Education of and for place carries an implication of stewardship of place as an aim. A middle school earth science teacher likely does not spend several months ensuring their students understand earth systems with the hope that those students will be able to pass a test, or even retain knowledge to pass a test far in the future. Rather, that educator more than likely dedicated their professional life toward the aim of inspiring their students to understand the earth on a meaningful level and to take actions, however defined, toward its preservation and conservation.

Although rarely explicitly stated, the ultimate outcome of teaching about and for place is action, not necessarily knowledge alone. More than likely there are existing goals related to conservation, preservation, or betterment of place in some kind. The reality is most educators teach with a hope of making their place better in some way, instead of just hoping that it can maintain the status quo.

The idea of teaching for civic engagement related to place is one well represented among approaches to place-based education.[1,2,3] However, these approaches, and the many others that can and should be created require a fundamental shift in how instruction is analyzed and assessed. The underlying assumption of most instruction related to place is that knowledge leads to action.

The oft repeated quote around many conservation education organizations from the Senegalese poet Baba Dioum is, "In the end, we will conserve only what we love, love only what we understand, and understand only what we are taught."[4] This assumption does invite a critical question that all educators of place must ask, "Does knowledge actually lead to action?" This assumption is well worth investigating as it is the cornerstone of many educational practices related to place.

The question of knowledge of place leading to action is one that has been addressed in the environmental education literature. One study that explored the connection found the environmental knowledge explained 2 percent of the variance in environmental behavior in fourth- to sixth-grade students.[5] For all practical purposes, the amount of knowledge related to the environment has no recognizable impact in fostering action toward the preservation or betterment of the environment. These findings mirror other studies.[6,7] The implications of the research are clear: The assumption that knowledge leads to action is deeply flawed.

In light of this research, it might be easy to start to think the teaching of place is a fool's errand. Although knowledge itself explained very little of the variation in action, there was another variable which was a much greater predictor: environmental connectedness. In these studies, the sense of connection to nature could predict around 70 percent of the variation in environmental behavior.

If a child, or adult, feels an emotional connection to nature or a place they are orders of magnitude more likely to take action for its betterment. If action is the ultimate aim in the teaching of place, the focal outcome in lessons or courses should be a sense of connectedness to the place, not knowledge alone. This is an outcome which challenges many existing assessment and evaluation structures in education.

With evidence that knowledge alone does not lead to action, it becomes curious to consider why the emphasis on knowledge as an outcome—or often, the outcome—persists. One influence which cannot be ignored is the pervasiveness of what Paolo Freire termed the "banking" concept of education.[8] In this model, students are containers to be filled with information by the teacher. Freire makes a compelling case for how this model is based on a rigid powerful dynamic between student and teacher and can be a powerful tool in oppression. Beyond these concerns, the emphasis of the passing of knowledge with the teaching of place carries several conveniences for educators.

In many ways, knowledge of place in the traditional educational content sense is much neater. This knowledge, whether accurate or not, carries a sense of objectivity and consistency. Connectedness as an aim is much more individualized and variable. Inviting a student to explore their community and share the particular connections they feel toward it requires a dialogue between teacher and student. Asking students to remember a list of local historical dates is much simpler. However, in this case the evidence is rather clear that the simpler practice is ultimately ineffective practice.

PURSUING CONNECTEDNESS IN
THE TEACHING OF PLACE

In recognizing connectedness as an outcome that has tremendous to potential to environmental action there are three critical questions to address: (1) What exactly is connectedness? (2) How is connectedness assessed? and (3) What types of experiences lead to connectedness? In addressing each of these questions, it is critical not to view them through the lens of how formal education is typically conducted, but rather to consider what opportunities exist to improve education toward this aim.

There are a handful of related concepts which can help in fully understanding what connectedness to place means. In many studies that have sought to explore this concept, connectedness has included appreciation of place, love for place, or a sense of oneness.[9] This attachment to and deep caring for place combined with understanding is referred to as "sense of place" in anthropology literature.[10] Arne Naess referred to this sensation as "belonging to a place."[11] Although these explanations are imprecise, the central point is that connectedness to a place involves individuals as not seeing themselves as completely distinct from the place itself.

The imprecision of the concept of connectedness also leads to challenges in assessing and evaluating connectedness. Many studies rely on some form of survey consisting of statements where participants indicate agreement or disagreement with a statement.[12] However, these instruments have a number of limitations when applied to educational settings. First, they are typically generalized and not content-specific. As a result, they might be used with regard to the impact of a course of an individual's connectedness to nature in general, but would not be appropriate for understanding connectedness to a particular topic related to place.

A second concern in many existing instruments is that they are vulnerable to individual interpretation of particular survey items. A word such as "nature" is very susceptible to individual interpretation. For example, a child who has grown up as a ranch may feel an intense connection to the local climate and grass, especially in how that affects their family's livelihood, but if they interpret "nature" to only mean park-type settings may indicate a low sense of connection. With large sample sizes these instruments can still be useful for research, but will be severely limited in understanding individual students' connectedness.

These concerns in assessment could prompt educators of place to revert back to more traditional evaluation of content-focused aims. However, as Elliot Eisner argues, a focus in evaluation reveals much about what educators truly value.[13] That is to say, reverting focus for sake of easier evaluation would indicate that actually teaching for the betterment of place was never that important to the teacher or school in the first place. Rather, this is just one example of how teaching for place requires a change in perspective to some of the fundamental practices of teaching.

Before addressing assessment, however, it is first important to better understand the types of experience which are likely to lead to connectedness. Again, research provides a lens into a number of factors which seem to impact connectedness.[14] Connectedness seems to generally be higher among young children and steadily declines, including during the school year. This indicates that connectedness is not just something which schools fail to promote, but rather something which schools actively lose.

A second factor, is the physical setting of the schools students attend. Students who attend schools in rural settings with presumably more or closer access to natural world (however conceived) tend to display higher connectedness. Two additional factors which contribute toward students' connectedness, and not in insignificant ways, are access to nature and mentors. The recognition of these two factors is ultimately the point where this transitions as a problem of practice for educators of place to a crisis.

The Crisis of Connectedness

Approaching any type of teaching with research-based evidence for the types of experiences which lead to a desired outcome seems like a position of strength for any educator. However, in understanding the changing backgrounds students bring to school, ensuring all students have access to the types of experiences necessary to develop connectedness to place is a decidedly uphill battle. These challenges are immense, even apart from those of the competing pressures on educators for instructional time.

In past generations, students brought experiences in nature with them to school. However, as Richard Louv outlined in his iconic work *Last Child in the Woods: Saving Our Children from Nature-Deficit Disorder*, the amount of time children spend interacting with nature has dropped precipitously.[15] He cites a study which indicated that between 1997 and 2003 the percentage of children engaging in outdoor activities declined by 50 percent. If connectedness to places, especially natural places, requires experience with that place, the evidence is resoundingly clear that most children do not have it.

As with any other need students have which is not being met outside of school, educators must now create these experiences compared to past decades when they may have been taken as a given. Moreover, where teaching to increase knowledge about a place combined with experience of the place might have led to increased connectedness, and often deeper understanding, students are no longer able to bring the experiences with them to pair with this instruction. Even experiences which educators might think of as being universal for children, such as climbing a tree, catching insects, or even visiting nearby state or national parks, are becoming increasingly rare.

Beyond the huge deficiency of experiences interacting with place, there is also a need to be concerned about access to mentors. As already discussed, these types of experiences have not generally been a point of emphasis in schools, and as a result the opportunities for teachers to serve as mentors in experiencing and exploring place are likely limited. Oftentimes, a mentor who guides a child in forming a connection to place is a family member, such as a parent. However, the timing of Louv's work creates a reason to be concerned in this area as well.

Louv's book originally published in 2005, meaning a twelve-year-old child at the time of his writing would be Millennials, which is the generation that are the parents of most students in elementary schools now. The generation which was already in crisis in terms of access to nature are now in the position that they would need to be serving as mentors for today's children. Beyond not having opportunities to experience nature, many children entering schools today may not have a mentor in their family to help them in these experiences even if they were to happen.

THE EXPERIENCE GAP

The evidence from the research could easily lead to a perception of the relationship between young people and the natural world as being one that is in constant and inevitable decline. It is not difficult to picture a sort of apocalyptic scene where the last child who plays outdoors goes extinct in a scene reminiscent of demise of the Wooly Mammoth. However, that is not actually the case. There are children who get rich and plentiful experiences with the natural world. However, which children get those experiences represents a matter of great inequality.

There are rather profound racial, income, and educational inequalities in which groups of children tend to have experiences in nature. Having a family history of spending time in nature, disposable income, and the educational background to feel confident in accessing natural areas are dramatic factors and represent significant barriers to large numbers of children never having a likely access to nature, even if there are technically access opportunities geographically near them. Moreover, skipping over the experience and interaction stage to focus on content further privileges students who are most likely to have the experiences which lead to connectedness.

MOVING FORWARD

In recognizing the importance of connectedness in prompting children toward action in the preservation of place and the deeply concerning decline in the set of existing experiences students bring to school, there is a pressing need for educators of place to reconceptualize what it means to teach about and for place. Existing approaches of emphasizing content-only or expecting students to come to school with enough experiences to form connections are not only unlikely to be meaningful over the long-term, but borderline delusional given the existing evidence.

Ultimately, educators seeking to improve their practice in the teaching of place cannot simply tweak or make small changes, but rather need to completely reconceptualize their work toward understanding how students form connections to place, and, most importantly, how those connections lead to action. The aim toward action as the goal in teaching for place is much more than application of learning; it is teaching for the explicit aim of improving place.

EXPANSIVE PLACE

In considering what it means to teach for the improvement of place from a conceptual perspective, it is worth taking a moment to consider the many different things "improving a place" could mean. On one level, it could be the preservation of a place so an individual or individuals can continue to experience it as they wish, such as preventing the construction of roads or mines in a historical site where an individual may visit. In which case, inspiring more individuals to join in that preservation has the potential to increase the potency of calls for preservation.

In another setting, improving place could be seeking to remove the impacts of environmental degradation. Perhaps a stream that flows through a community is heavily polluted by the overuse of pesticides and herbicides on lawns. With enough activism, a group of people or students could petition the city council to change regulations or even appeal to individuals to change habits which could lead to an increase in environmental quality.

However, an even broader perspective which will be explored in chapters ahead is to back out and consider all of the different things a place can be and can mean, and aim to expand it. In practice this is not just aiming to get students involved in an existing cause, but to develop and contribute their perspective of a place more broadly. Conceptually, the goal is not to preserve or improve a place as is, but to use education as a tool to expand what it means.

REFLECTION QUESTIONS

1. With what places do you feel a sense of connectedness? What does this connection mean to you, and how has it influence who you are as a person?
2. What evaluation structures and practices are present in your teaching? How might these structures promote or limit considerations of place?
3. Which students with whom you work are privileged in terms of opportunities to experience place and which are not?
4. In what ways would you like to see your local place improve? What opportunities are there to connect these improvements to your teaching practice?

NOTES

1. Amy B. Demarest, *Place-Based Curriculum Design: Exceeding Standards Through Local Investigations* (New York: Routledge, 2015).

2. Sarah K. Anderson, *Bringing Life to School: Place-Based Education Across the Curriculum* (Lanham, MD: Rowman & Littlefield, 2017).

3. David Greenwood and Gregory A. Smith, *Place-Based Education in the Global Age: Local Diversity* (New York: Routledge, 2008).

4. University of Wisconsin, "Society for Ecological Restoration Gallery," Society for Ecological Restoration UW, accessed October 25, 2022, https://sites.uw.edu/seruw/gallery/.

5. Siegmar Otto and Pamela Pensini. "Nature-Based Environmental Education of Children: Environmental Knowledge and Connectedness to Nature, Together, Are Related to Ecological Behaviour." *Global Environmental Change 47* (2017): 88–94.

6. Pihui Liu, Teng Minmin, and Han Chuanfeng. "How Does Environmental Knowledge Translate into Pro-Environmental Behaviors?: The Mediating Role of Environmental Attitudes and Behavioral Intentions." *The Science of the Total Environment 728* (2020): 138126.

7. Miles Richardson, Holli-Anne Passmore, Lea Barbett, Ryan Lumber, Rory Thomas, and Alex Hunt. "The Green Care Code: How Nature Connectedness and Simple Activities Help Explain Pro-Nature Conservation Behaviours." *People and Nature 2*, no. 3 (2020): 821–39.

8. Paulo Freire, *Pedagogy of the Oppressed* (Harmondsworth, UK: Penguin Education, 1972).

9. Louise Chawla. "Childhood Nature Connection and Constructive Hope: A Review of Research on Connecting with Nature and Coping with Environmental Loss." *People and Nature 2*, no. 3 (2020): 619–42.

10. Steven Feld and Keith H. Basso, *Senses of Place* (Santa Fe, NM: School of American Research Press, 2015).

11. Arne Naess, *Ecology of Wisdom*, trans. Alan Drengson and Bill Devall (London: Penguin Classics, 2016).

12. Eluned Price, Sarah Maguire, Catherine Firth, Ryan Lumber, Miles Richardson, and Richard Young. "Factors Associated with Nature Connectedness in School-Aged Children." *Current Research in Ecological and Social Psychology 3* (2022): 100037.

13. Elliot W. Eisner, *The Enlightened Eye* (Upper Saddle River, NJ: Prentice Hall, 1994).

14. Eluned Price, Sarah Maguire, Catherine Firth, Ryan Lumber, Miles Richardson, and Richard Young. "Factors Associated with Nature Connectedness in School-Aged Children." *Current Research in Ecological and Social Psychology 3* (2022): 100037.

15. Richard Louv, *Last Child in the Woods* (Chapel Hill, NC: Algonquin Books, 2008).

Chapter 4

The Person in Place

A first teaching job is always a scary and exciting experience, and I could not have been more excited when I accepted my position late one spring at a parochial school in nearby Joplin, Missouri. I was hired to teach sixth- through eighth-grade science. The sixth graders would study general science and health, seventh grade focused and life science, and eighth grade addressed earth and space, including one of my favorite middle school science topics: weather.

However, on a Sunday afternoon in May, three months before I would start teaching, how my students and I would both view weather suddenly and dramatically changed as an EF-5 tornado ripped its way through the city. Although seeing the devastation was difficult, weather remained for me as it had always been: a fascinating academic subject to explore. For some of my students, however, it became something very different.

Weather was not content; it was the thing that destroyed their home, the thing that gutted their community, and even the thing that killed some of their loved ones. Local weather as a topic was no longer just something with which my students and I had different levels of experience, knowledge, or comfort. Rather, local weather was something fundamentally different for me, the science teacher, and my students who had just survived a tornado.

One of the great innovators in landscape photography was Bradford Washburn.[1] Among his innovations were the incorporation of flight to gain a higher perspective of mountains and the inclusion of an element intentionally excluded among other influential photographers, Ansel Adams included: humans. Washburn typically included human figures to provide a sense of scale in his work. He used the small dot of a mountaineer to allow the viewer to truly appreciate the vastness of places such as the Alaska Range. The humans did not appear in contrast to the grandness of the place, but rather to better convey that sense to the viewer.

THE HUMAN ELEMENT

At the simplest level, connectedness as an aim in the teaching of place contains two elements: the person and the place. In many cases, place in this equation consists of the content, especially in natural and social sciences. However, focusing exclusively on this aspect ignores a critical element in the person themselves. To parody a proverbial question, "If a tree falls in a forest and no human is there to experience it, is a connection made?" Obviously, the answer to this hypothetical is a resounding "no." Truly understanding the connection between a person and place requires an understanding of the person in the place.

There has been a large amount of research around the psychological perspectives of humans' experience in place, particularly natural places.[2] There are also numerous documented health benefits to time in natural places.[3] Although these perspectives are interesting and could certainly provide reasons for educators and schools to be intentional about increasing students' contact time with place, they are not the most useful for questions of teaching practice. Ultimately when it comes to curricula, the key lens is not psychological or biological, but epistemological.

KNOWING PLACE

To truly explore how humans come to know a specific place or place more broadly is an endeavor that could fill many volumes, and indeed already has. The aim in this discussion is not to divine a single, unifying explanation of how a human knows a place, but rather to explore what perspectives of this process are most useful in guiding curricular and educational decisions. Ultimately, all organisms know their environment to a certain extent.[4] However, for educators of place, how humans come to know a place in particular ways is really the critical question.

An additional challenge in exploring an epistemology of place for educators is that in some ways this falls well within more mainstream educational epistemologies such as behaviorism or constructivism, but in other ways is quite different. A critical difference is that where education in many areas is bound both in time and scope, the learning of place is often not. An algebra teacher's students might experience their content outside of the classroom, but a teacher seeking to help their students know their community better will definitely have those students interacting with that subject constantly.

Similarly, in many subject areas, teachers might be able to control the scope of their students' learning. Reading teachers are able to ensure their students are reading materials which are developmentally appropriate and it is highly unlikely that reading materials beyond this scope will suddenly appear before the students. However, in the teaching of place, the place itself might alter the scope of learning. An exploration of local native plants could be, suddenly and dramatically, interrupted by a change in weather. Teachers for most subjects may be able to control how their students experience content, but teachers of place, for the most part, cannot.

An additional challenge in considering how students experience place is that ultimately that experience has to be considered on multiple conceptual levels. First, experiences in place are filtered through the lens of the perceived role of humans with regards to place. As Aldo Leopold argued with regards to ecosystems, a shift from viewing humans as conquerors of a place, to members of the community prompts vastly different actions.[5]

The important point is not that different perspectives lead to different actions, but that these different actions would be justified based on the perspectives. However, many of the perspectives that are often discussed carry an assumption that is counterproductive to more clearly understanding how students form an understanding of place. These perspectives assume that place is an objective entity, but Arne Naess makes a compelling argument for the potential dangers in this assumption.[6]

Treating a place as objective and fixed might on the surface seem to be a safe assumption. Taking a small forest in a city park as an example, the trees, animals, soil, and other elements do all physically exist. If a student visits this park they may describe many characteristics of the trees such as tall, green, and rough. Some students might even extend their description of the trees to include characteristics such as peaceful or majestic or more particular descriptions such as identifying the trees as lodgepole pines.

As discussed by Naess, many of some of these characteristics seem objective and a product of the place, while others seem subjective and a product of the person.[7] However, many characteristics that are often considered objective are in fact ascribed by the human. In that light, what might be taught as objective related to a place might in fact be a matter of the educator's perspective. Objectivity related to place is a very difficult, if not often impossible, goal to pursue in educational practice.

To revisit the hypothetical city park forest, three characteristics that could be described of the trees are the needles are green, the bark is rough, and the tree is a lodgepole pine. A characteristic such as rough is a bit easier to recognize as being a product of a human, but the other characteristics very much are as well. Describing a tree as green relies on the interpretation of light by the human eye and the recognition of a color as "green." Although most visitors to the forest would likely also describe the trees as green, an image of a dress well circulated on the internet clearly demonstrated that different viewers can have very different perceptions of color.

Additionally, the label of lodgepole pine seems to be objective. However, identifying a tree as a particular species is accomplished through human-created systems of classification which ascribes a particular label to a tree appearing to have a particular set of characteristics. The revisions of these labels and systems by taxonomists are a clear indication that although systematic, identification of a species is not in fact objective.

Although considering this discussion of the person in place might seem detached from the reality of teaching practices, it highlights the need for a key conceptual shift. Rather than viewing humans as objects or organisms which visit or exist in an objective place, it is necessary to recognize that humans are in fact the instrument which interprets place. Through this interpretation, humans not only experience place, but in those experiences, they create meaning and value in those places through their interpretation.

BEING IN PLACE

Recognizing that place is understood by filtering experience through the lens of human interpretation leads to a critical aspect of teaching for place. That is to say a place, as it is understood by an individual is different than as experienced and understood by another. This is not a matter of perspective, but as Naess argued, a "difference . . . of ontology."[8] Stated differently, in experiencing place, individuals create a meaning or an understanding that is their own. As place is always understood through human interaction and experiences, places are, as a result, simultaneously many things at once.

This plurality creates a unique challenge for educators of place. Whereas with other subjects, students might bring different perspectives to a lesson, with place, the subject can be fundamentally different to each of them. As a matter of example, in a rural community, to one student the surrounding landscape might be an agricultural area which allows their family to make a living and to another it could be a quaint retreat from busier metropolitan life. To yet another student, the area could be land where their family hunts. All of these iterations not only coexist, but will be brought together in the classroom.

The critical necessity for educators of place is to recognize that diminishing one interpretation of a place also carries personal weight for the student. It is not a matter of correcting misconceptions as educators might do with other content, as challenging an understanding of place has implications for students' understandings of themselves and their families. Additionally, although students may share having experienced a place, including their own community, they could have constructed varied understandings of the place.

THE EDUCATOR IN PLACE

Ultimately, as educators of place, the aim is to translate a conceptual under-standing of how individuals come to know and understand place into practice. Although there are curricular and pedagogical considerations, the implica-tions of this lens expand into other elements of teaching practice. The three points of focus for educators need to be to (1) come to know and understand their own places, (2) consider how their understandings of place will shape their curricular and pedagogical decisions, and (3) design instruction to sup-port the plurality of meanings of place.

In recognizing that understanding of place is constructed through human experience and interpretation it is essential for educators of place to engage with place themselves. Through their own engagement with place, educators can create a repository of experience they can use in guiding students through sense-making. Alternatively, how can educators coach students through developing an understanding of place if they have not done so themselves? Whereas educator professional development tends to focus on classroom practice, educators of place must also seek to expand their own connection and understanding of place itself.

As educators seek to expand their own connection to place there are a num-ber of issues for them to consider. First, understanding of place is constructed through experience and interaction with place, not by the memorization of facts of ideas related to the place. Although there are many ways educators can engage with place, it is essential that they engage in a manner that is interactive rather than being passive recipients of information.

Second, educators, especially those who focus on a particular content area, tend to focus on engaging with place through the lens of their content area. To build a deeper understanding of place, it would be beneficial to step outside of that content area to understand other directions of inquiry. An earth sci-ence teacher who expands to experience the history of a place or a literature teacher which engages with an ecosystem both will have a richer understand-ing of place than if they had continued in their content area alone.

Educators must also consider places with which they should engage to better practice their craft of teaching. To gain experience in interacting with and interpreting particular places, it is beneficial for educators to have inter-acted with those places themselves. Although this seems fairly intuitive with content-specific locations, such as historical sites, there are other locations that could be critical for educators in their practice. Specifically, it is essential for educators to understand the places in which they teach and where their students live.

Particularly for educators who may be relatively new to the communities in which they teach, to guide students through the experience of interpreting and coming to know that place, they must have first had that experience themselves. Moreover, it provides a much greater framework for understanding and predicting how experiences with place impact students. Potentially, there could also be a need for educators to engage with the neighborhoods and communities in which their students live if that differs from their own. This could be particularly relevant for schools that serve large geographic areas.

There are a number of examples of educators who engaged deeply with place, with more famous examples among naturalists such as John Muir and Enos Mills. Arne Naess himself engaged famously with place at his home Tvergastein, as well abroad, including Himalayan expeditions. Although these prominent examples demonstrate a nearly lifelong, immersive engagement with place, there are a number of practices which fit more neatly into busy schedules and can help educators understand their own identity in place.

Finally, educators must engage with place with the aim of understanding it better. In his insightful book *Ecological Identity: Becoming a Reflective Environmentalist*, Mitchell Thomashow provides a number of activities which educators can use in reflecting on their own connection to the places around them.[9] One that has a particular opportunity to help educators uncover aspects of engaging with place where they may be lacking is called the community network map. The activity consists of a number of reflective questions related to the networks and connections which exist in a community.

As educators reflect on the connections in their community it is important to recognize that all individuals are in fact members of many communities at many different levels. Beyond considering the networks of a community in terms of a town or neighborhood, there is also an opportunity to consider a school or classroom as a community on a smaller scale. Additionally, educators are members of ecological communities consisting of many species. In exploring each of these levels, it is likely that any educators will find aspects of the connections that they do not fully understand.

CONCLUSION

It can be tempting when preparing to teach about place to focus on the place itself as content. However, the humans involved in the actual teaching, the educator and the students, are themselves lenses which drastically impact how place is understood. In this consideration, the teaching of place is a process which is very personalized to individual educators, students, and communities. As a result, it is essential to design lessons about place for their specific students.

REFLECTION QUESTIONS

1. What formative experiences have you had with place? How do these shape language and perspectives you bring to exploring and connecting with other places?
2. With what specific places or types of places do you not have experience? How could increasing your experience with those places impact your teaching practice?
3. What perceptions or lenses do you tend to use in interpreting place? What could those lenses reveal? What might those lenses conceal?

NOTES

1. American Alpine Club, "Washburn Remembered," *American Alpine Journal*, 2007, https://aac-publications.s3.amazonaws.com/documents/aaj/2007/PDF/AAJ _2007_49_81_106.pdf.

2. Byeongsang Oh, Kyung Ju Lee, Chris Zaslawski, Albert Yeung, David Rosenthal, Linda Larkey, and Michael Back. "Health and Well-Being Benefits of Spending Time in Forests: Systematic Review." *Environmental Health and Preventive Medicine* 22, no. 1 (2017): 71.

3. Howard Frumkin, Gregory N. Bratman, Sara Jo Breslow, Bobby Cochran, Peter H. Kahn Jr., Joshua J. Lawler, Phillip S. Levin, Pooja S. Tandon, Usha Varanasi, Kathleen L. Wolf, and Spencer A. Wood. "Nature Contact and Human Health: A Research Agenda." *Environmental Health Perspectives 125*, no. 7 (2017): 075001.

4. J. A. A. Swart, "Towards an Epistemology of Place," in *New Visions of Nature: Complexity and Authenticity*, ed. Martin Drenthen, Jozef Keulartz, and James D. Proctor (Dordrecht, NL: Springer, 2009), pp. 197–203.

5. Aldo Leopold, *A Sand County Almanac* (Baraboo, WI: Land Ethic Press; The Aldo Leopold Foundation, 2007).

6. Arne Naess, *Ecology of Wisdom*, trans. Alan Drengson and Bill Devall (London: Penguin Classics, 2016).

7. Naess, *Ecology of Wisdom*.

8. Naess, *Ecology of Wisdom*, 77.

9. Mitchell Thomashow, *Ecological Identity: Becoming a Reflective Environmentalist* (Cambridge, MA: MIT Press, 1996).

Chapter 5

Public Places and Spaces

"Climb up this side of the gate," I tell my six-year-old son as he hikes up an oversized camouflage t-shirt as if it were a Victorian dress. We are accessing a few hundred acres of state land during the early days of dove season. Although I grew up in the outdoors, I did not grow up hunting. It was an activity I was trying to self-teach in order to help my children better understand the connection of how they get food.

"WHAT!?!?!" my son shouted back. The lack of volume awareness paired with his oversized hearing protection had my son speaking at a volume, which suffices to say, would not have pleased Elmer Fudd. Thanks to novice abilities, our impact on the animals that day did not exceed scaring a few so they moved to a different corner of the property, but I hoped a bit of the overall aim of the lesson would stick.

Ultimately, the opportunity only existed because of the piece of public land available. I do not, nor does anyone in my family, own large pieces of land. Our sum total family expanses of land represent a few residential lawns. Despite not owning huge tracts of land, my son and I were able to engage with the landscape in a completely new way.

Starting from an understanding of the role humans play in interpreting and ascribing meaning to place, it only seems logical to consider that process would play out differently with different types of places, and undoubtedly it does. This process is highly individualized, and variations in place will certainly make a difference. However, beyond variabilities in the process of making sense of place, there are critical differences in the implications of how individuals make sense of place for different types of places.

The variability in implications does not necessarily have to do with the type of landscape, population level, ecology, or similar characteristics of place, but with the ownership and governance structures of that place. It is generally acceptable that with particular places such as a family's home, the members of that family are free to ascribe meaning and value to that place, and that meaning should probably supersede the meaning of an individual who happens to drive by the house. At the very least, the meaning and values of the homeowners should be the ones that direct decisions related to the care and management of the home.

Although this balance seems intuitive for places which are privately held and intended primarily for private use, vast numbers of locations are not. Many places are either specifically held by the public, such as in the case of public lands, while others are intended for public use, such as a museum, even if technically privately owned. In these cases, engagement with the place is not simply a matter of better understanding the place itself, or even using the place as an avenue to better understand particular content. Rather, engagement with public places is really a matter of democratic participation.

To truly unwind the implications of educators inviting and empowering students to engage with public places, there are two critical elements. First, it is necessary to consider not only what is a public place and the characteristics of a place that is publicly held. Second, and no less important, educators must understand how these public places are constructed socially. Ultimately, the aim of educating for public places should be that students are not just intellectually aware of these places, but also socially prepared to engage in shaping their direction.

PUBLIC PLACES

Public places can vary widely from schools, small city parks, all the way to the hundreds of millions of acres of designated public lands in the United States. Complicating matters further, there are places which are operated as a public service, such as a post office or governmental office, but which in some way feel very different in terms of educational implications. To make the distinction between which types of publicly held places are critical for considering in teaching for place, it is helpful to consider Don Mitchell's term "space of representation."[1]

A space of representation, according to Mitchell, is "a place in which groups and individuals can make themselves visible." In these spaces individuals and groups are able to make their desires seen. As a matter of example, consider an artist sketching in a city park. By going into a public place, the artist is making visible to others their desire to engage with a place through their drawing. They also, more than likely, are expressing a desire that places which are open to the public and allow for such activities should continue to exist.

In a similar light, the millions of visitors who enter national parks each year, no matter which activities they pursue in those parks, clearly communicate a desire for such places to exist and be visible. Although these parks might often be thought of as consumptive locations, as in where someone goes to "take in" nature, they are in fact places where individuals are able to make their desire to experience natural places visible. An individual who desires to better understand and appreciate plants can read and study in private, but entering into a space of representation makes that desire visible to others.

Making one's desires visible is not just a matter of expression, but of societal equity. As mentioned before, in a private space, such as an individual's home, their perspectives and desires for that place are prioritized and weighted. Similarly, they can use that private space to express their desires, a phenomenon clearly visible during election years as campaign signs appear across suburban lawns. Additionally, some individuals may because of their status be afforded additional private spaces to express their desires, such as an office, private club, or theatre.

However, those without access to such private spaces must rely on public places to express their desires. This means that public spaces are a powerful tool for equity because they, at least in theory, allow all individuals regardless of economic or social privilege to make their needs and desires visible. Without such places, this form of expression becomes limited to only those who are economically able to support their act of expression.

Although Mitchell made critical arguments for how the restriction of public places can have an extremely adverse impact on vulnerable populations such as the homeless, the concept expands much more broadly and across social groups. For example, an individual may wish to start hunting to be able to harvest their own meat rather than purchase the products of industrial agriculture. An individual who is wealthy, or has the necessary social connections, might purchase large pieces of land, or gain access to those pieces of land in order to pursue that desire. They could then pursue their desire to hunt and communicate that desire to others in stories.

Needing to acquire large amounts of land, or at least access to the land, would represent a nearly insurmountable barrier for most people of more modest means who might wish to pursue that desire. However, public lands offer a critical resource for equitable access, and by extension, equitable opportunity to make one's desires visible. By being generally accessible to all individuals (within the scope of relevant regulations), public lands provide a guaranteed space of representation for this desire, as well as countless others.

Public lands in the United States consist of lands managed for public use by municipal, state, and federal governments. At the federal level, these lands typically fall under the National Parks Service, United States Forest Service, and the Bureau of Land Management and represent over 600 million acres.[2] Most of these lands include in their official designation the phrase "for the benefit and enjoyment of the people." These lands are also managed for multiple use, so in many cases recreational activities such as hiking or camping are balanced with uses such as grazing, mining, and oil and gas extraction.

A critical distinction for federal public lands is that they are managed for the benefit and enjoyment of all Americans, not just those that live nearby. Moreover, they are held in the public trust with all Americans serving as equal joint owners of vast reserve of intellectual, emotional, spiritual, and, not to be excluded, financial wealth. Although this vast resource is publicly held and all Americans technically have equal shares, they do not all have equal preparation and opportunity to engage in representing their desires for these lands.

Ultimately, the concern of equitable opportunity to engage with public places is not just a matter of representation for visibility's sake, but a matter of democratic involvement. Although these places are typically managed by professionals for the day-to-day operations and oversight, the larger question of what these lands mean and what values and desires should be weighted is one that should fall to the populous as a whole. However, this sort of engagement is one that requires an understanding of one's own ownership and stake in these lands, as well as the tools, skills, and knowledge to participate in directing these lands.

Although increasing democratic participation is a pressing educational need across many contexts, the challenges in increasing this participation related to public lands play out slightly differently. Political skills and knowledge, such as how to vote and communicate with legislatures and government officials, are obviously important, but perhaps a more significant barrier to preparing students to engage with public places is not just failing to teach particular skills, but rather the way in which those places are presented in educational settings as a whole.

PRODUCTION OF PLACE

A critical shortcoming in teaching related to place, and one that is particularly devastating in the case of public places, is that place is presented as an object. Across a range of subject areas, places are discussed as entities which can be understood with definable characteristics, and often these lessons carry an aura of objectivity. These places are then understood to be the setting in which people currently live, have lived in the past, or are incapable of living depending on the topic and example.

However, this method of presentation is very reductionist. Climate, geology, ecology, history, sociology, and politics can fill in some aspects of the picture, but none can do all. More importantly, the total of what a place is and can be exceeds even what sum of those individual perspectives. More importantly, as Henri Lefebvre argued, the idea of any of these isolated perspectives is really an abstraction.[3] That is to say, the idea of only looking at the geology of a place, without considering the human history, ecology, climate, and many other aspects is a perspective which only exists in the mind, but not on the physical planet.

Places necessarily consist of many coexisting elements, individuals, and relationships, all constantly interacting. Isolating any element can provide useful insights, but an appreciation of the place as a whole requires recognizing the wide range of components both known and unknown that contribute toward the place itself. The leads to the critical revelation that place is not an object but a product. Places are not only made but often remade through an iterative process.

Lefebvre referred to the product, or outcome, of place as an *oeuvre*. Borrowed from his native French, an oeuvre is a composition, such as a work of art. However, from Lefebvre's perspective, the key distinction with place is that it is a composition in which all of its citizens participate. As a work of art, engagement in place takes on a meaning that then extends beyond typical civic participation. In a democracy, participation is often thought of in terms of expressing opinions and beliefs and prompting representative and government officials to execute those desires. With place, people are not constituents; they are co-creators.

Applying this perspective to public places in particular, engagement with these places in its purest sense would be participating in the production of their meaning, value, and understanding. The goal for students is not just to equip them to better understand particular content related to a place, but to be able to participate in the production of what that public place is. The risk in not doing so is that not the public places themselves will remain undefined, but that they will only be defined by a small minority of individuals who will then impose that meaning of the place on everyone.

EDUCATION AND OEUVRE

In considering the role of education with the oeuvre, the work of art that is place, the concern is not that education has not taken a role. Places are the products of a number of social processes, and undoubtedly education as a social process is included. Education already contributes toward the collective understanding of what place is. The need for reflection then comes in considering if the compositions that are these public places reflect the values and aims for which educators would wish.

Public land usage represents some rather remarkable racial inequalities.[4] Although there have been more recent trends toward more diverse populations utilizing public lands, the clear evidence in the outcome of the place is that not all groups of people feel equally able to access and utilize these places. Similarly, recent threats of eliminating, selling, or removing restrictions on public lands by politicians indicate there is not a clear perception that those actions will be widely opposed.[5] Disproportionately doing such actions with lands which are significant to Indigenous communities also reveals a lack of broad resistance to inclusion in these lands.

The aim in highlighting these concerns with public lands is not to say that education is explicitly to blame, but to recognize that education related to place, as is currently practiced, has been a component in the creation of this inequitable version of these places. Stated differently, although education may not have explicitly caused the injustices related to public places, it certainly has not prevented them. In many ways, this is likely due to the tendency of education to focus on, what Edward Soja called, the opaque elements of place.[6] That is, education has focused on the surface level elements of place, without introducing the necessary transparency.

Transparency in the teaching of place allows for considering the individual element, such as climate or history, but then looking through that element to see how it interacts with the viewer as well as others who inhabit or visit the place. Transparency also invites the student to look through the elements of place to try to better understand themselves. Although this is certainly more complex than only teaching surface-level concepts, it is necessary to truly equip students to engage with place.

Furthermore, teaching only the surface elements of place is teaching a simulacrum of place, but not place itself. Teaching place must include many angles, perspectives, lenses, and human elements because ultimately that is what the place is. By compressing place into smaller elements, teaching becomes simpler, but ultimately what is taught is no longer the place itself. This reduction is much the same as the display of Egyptian artifacts and mummies revealing some insights about the Pyramids, but no longer being the Pyramids themselves.

In short, teaching for public places must shift from a focus on the acquisition and retention of the superficial to fully preparing students to engage in creation of these works of art. That includes engaging to represent their own perspective, as well as advocating for the perspectives of those who are not represented. In educational settings, that will also mean adapting approaches to teaching that allow students to expand, explore, and create perspectives of place that extend beyond that of the teacher and those in curricula. This is teaching focused on transforming students into artists.

REFLECTION QUESTIONS

1. What public places are significant for your students? Do all students have equal access to these places and/or what factors could be limiting access?
2. In what ways could you replicate elements of public places within your classroom or school?
3. How might "spaces of representation" be created in the school setting?
4. What elements of your curriculum or teaching practice are opaque related to place? In what ways could you introduce transparency to these elements?

NOTES

1. Don Mitchell, *The Right to the City: Social Justice and the Fight for Public Space* (New York: The Guilford Press, 2014).

2. John D. Leshy, *Our Common Ground: A History of America's Public Lands* (New Haven, CT: Yale University Press, 2022).

3. Henri Lefebvre, *The Production of Space*, trans. Donald Nicholson-Smith (Malden, MA: Blackwell, 2009).

4. Audrey Peterman and Frank Peterman, *Legacy on the Land: A Black Couple Discovers Our National Inheritance and Tells Why Every American Should Care* (Atlanta, GA: Earthwise Productions, 2009).

5. David Gessner, *Leave It As It Is: A Journey Through Theodore Roosevelt's American Wilderness* (New York: Simon & Schuster, 2020).

6. Edward W. Soja, *Postmodern Geographies: The Reassertion of Space in Critical Social Theory* (London, UK: Verso, 2011).

Chapter 6

Emplacement in Teaching

As a science educator, I am often shared anecdotes about different activities, lessons, and curricula. Those are also the elements that most often draw my attention anytime I visit a school building. That is why I was particularly struck by an announcement I overheard while visiting a rural school located on the short-grass high plains.

"Please attend the fundraiser for our reforestation project." I did a bit of a mental double take and missed the details of when and where the fundraiser was taking place. Reforestation, I assumed by definition, meant that a place had once previously been a forest. On the semiarid plains, this could not be further from the truth.

I decided to ask a few questions in the school to learn more about the project. One teacher shared with me that the project was part of a unit in their curriculum related to human impacts on ecosystems. I asked what the curriculum was and found that its authors were from the Bay Area in California. I could not help but think that those authors were not thinking of dust bowl country when they designed this unit.

In truly recognizing the complexities of place as a socially created composition, it can be overwhelming to consider how such a truly broad concept can be integrated into a single course. Similarly, even if a teacher feels that including place for a few special projects or on particular days does not do it justice, it can still be very difficult to see how to include place more while still addressing necessary content. However, a key shift in perspective can provide an alternative to these struggles. The important question is not how an educator fits place into their content, but rather situates their content within place.

The act of situating teaching in place, or emplacement, sits at a crossroads of two conceptual perspectives. The first of these perspectives is philosophical and deals with the role of emplacement in creating and communicating meaning. The second is geographical and addresses how the act of emplacement leads to justice and injustice. Although these lenses are not strictly tied

37

to each other, it can be helpful to think of them as two continua which comprise a coordinate plane. With regards to the philosophical lens, emplacement ranges from meaningful to irrelevant. For the geographical, the extremes are equity and exclusivity.

Before addressing these two axes, it is first important to recognize that emplacement is not an additional action educators can take to improve their practice. Rather, it is an implicit action in all teaching. Teaching and learning always occur somewhere. Even in distance learning, students and educators are physically located somewhere, although those places might not be the same. Despite the continued push toward standardized, placeless curricula, the act of teaching will always take place somewhere.

MEANING THROUGH EMPLACEMENT

Before understanding how meaning arises through emplacement, it is helpful to first understand alternative explanations of how words get their meaning. One alternative would be having an authority that clearly decides what a word does and does not mean. Although this might be common with regards to particular terms in legal documents, this is obviously not the case for the vast majority of day-to-day conversations. On the other extreme, it would be possible to think that the meaning of words is completely relative and that each person can choose for themselves what they mean.

Although relativism might seem more inclusive, it creates a significant problem in that it impedes actual communication. Ludwig Wittgenstein argued for the importance in agreement for meaning to be communicated.[1] Practically, this means that a person saying a word or phrase offers a meaning, but the listener must agree with that offering in order for communication to occur. Essentially, the speaker and listener must apply the same judgement to the topic. Consider the following possible classroom example:

> TEACHER: *The geology of Yosemite was greatly impacted by glaciation which was in the recent history. In fact, a lot of features, such as many lakes, did not exist in Yosemite before the glaciation.*
>
> STUDENT: *Are there any pictures that were taken before there were lakes?*
>
> TEACHER: *No, that was a long time before any humans were there, let alone cameras.*
>
> STUDENT: *But I thought you said it was recent?*

A misunderstanding such as this is all too common for geology teachers. The obvious issue at hand is that the student and teacher did not agree in their judgement of what constitutes recent. More importantly, neither the student or teacher's assessment of "recent" are wrong. In geologic time, glaciation which occurred two to three million years ago is recent. For a student who has grown up during the information age and 24-hour news cycle, recent becomes considerably less time ago.

Stanley Cavell described this characteristic of language by saying, " . . . the saying of something when and as it is said is as significant as the meaning and ordering of the words said."[2] In the example, the issue was not that the teacher was imprecise in their language, but rather that the teacher did not consider the setting and perspective in which the student was receiving the information and the meaning which they were likely to infer as a result.

The traditional educational response to this miscommunication might be to more explicitly teach vocabulary. However, that falls short in a few regards. First, the term that was misunderstood was not academic vocabulary, but rather an everyday word which carried a different meaning in this context. Second, and more importantly, the goal of the discussion was not the definition of a particular word, but rather to understand what it means for a landscape to be reshaped by geologic forces. Although the teacher understood the geologic concept, they fell short of understanding the context in which the student received the information.

As a mechanism for addressing these disagreements in judgements, Gottlieb described "mutual teaching" as "go over the rules in light of the situation, and go over the situation in light of the rules."[3] Stated differently, the teacher must be clear in communicating what they mean in describing the topic in a particular way, but must also be willing to learn from the student the perspectives and experiences they are bringing to an understanding. The ultimate issue is that the teacher must not take for granted that they know what an idea means universally and must instead be willing to work with their students to understand what it means in their classroom.

The essential point for educators to recognize is that students do not construct meaning by receiving and retaining information; they construct meaning by seeing how a concept is experienced in the places in which they live and learn. If educators fail to engage in "mutual teaching" students may still be able to retain information related to an idea, but it is very unlikely that those lessons will actually lead to the creation of any meaning. Consider another example from a preschool curriculum developed in an urban setting, but taught in a rural setting.[4]

TEACHER: *Alright class, we are going to have a class discussion. Our essential question is "How does my community use various modes of transportation?" So what kinds of transportation do you use?*

STUDENT 1: My mom brings me to school in a minivan.

STUDENT 2: My dad drops me off in a truck.

In the curriculum for the example there are a number of other possibilities listed that students might suggest such as a subway, metrocard, taxi, or train. In an extremely rural community, none of these options exist. However, to engage in "mutual teaching" as Gottlieb suggested, the lesson can gain increased meaning. The "rule" outlined implied in the curriculum is that transportation deals mainly with moving people. In an urban setting with a large number of people this makes sense. However, in a rural setting transportation deals much more with moving goods.

Asking students "What transportation do you use?" will likely divulge into discussing makes and models of passenger vehicles. However, in considering goods produced or extracted in rural communities to ask "What forms of transportation do you see around our community?" In a farming community, crops are likely harvested by a combine harvester, transferred to a grain cart pulled by a tractor, and transferred again from the grain cart to a grain truck or semitruck. This truck will likely transport the grain to a grain elevator where later it will be loaded onto train cars.

In this example, the first discussion would lead to students recognizing that different people use different types of vehicles. However, the second question opens up a consideration of how transportation occurs in different forms and connects people across long distances. The meaning found in that discussion also begins to lay the foundation for considering how their rural community interacts with other rural communities and metropolitan areas around them.

The key takeaway for teachers is that the focus on the action of emplacement led to a better lesson in terms of the subject area itself. At times, educators might think that a consideration of place is just a way for some content areas to do a favor for geography, history, or environmental science teachers. However, the reality is that an intentional emplacement of content within a particular setting leads to a deeper understanding and richer meaning of the content itself for students.

Ultimately, the physical classroom, school, and community are not just where students make sense of place, it is where they ascribe meaning to all content. Although students might be able to retain information related to the water cycle from a generic diagram in a textbook, they only truly ascribe meaning to the concept when they see how precipitation, runoff, and extraction of water play out in their surroundings. In short, content is only an idea until placed within the context of students' lived experience.

EQUITY IN EMPLACEMENT

The second axis along which to consider the emplacement of teaching deals with equity and justice. Soja coined the term spatial justice to describe the "outcomes of countless decisions about emplacement, where things are put in space."[5] An essential point of emphasis in this definition is that justice or injustice with regards to emplacement is the result of decisions, and is not somehow inherent. "It's just geography" is an oft repeated excuse to explain spatial injustices, such as a lack of access to healthcare or educational facilities. However, that perspective ignores that in those cases a lack of access is the result of human decisions.

Much of Soja's work focused on the placement of various physical facilities within urban landscapes and the injustices which resulted therefrom. However, it is not unreasonable to extend this lens to consider justices and injustices that could arise from decisions made during emplacement in other contexts. Applied to education, the emplacement of curricula within individual classrooms, schools, and communities is absolutely the result of a number of human decisions. Moreover, it is not unreasonable to consider that such emplacement can result in justice or injustice.

Essentially, if educators believe that a curriculum can be unjust, or that it can support the perpetuation of injustices, the decision made in emplacing that curriculum can and does contribute toward justice or lack thereof. In short, emplacement is not a neutral act. It is a key feature of a much deeper understanding of what constitutes place. This moves beyond thinking of place as simply context and instead to considering place, in Soja's words, as "socially-based."[6] It is an understanding of place that arises from engaging in the listening better to which Cavell called.[7]

EMPLACEMENT ANALYSIS FRAMEWORK

Ultimately the struggle in considering the two axes of emplacement is not in conceptualizing either access, but rather in considering how individual classroom practices or curricula relate to either axis and where they fit on the axis. More importantly, there is the need not to decipher the absolute position of a particular approach to teaching, but rather to consider the relative positions. Rather than use this framework to determine if a practice meets minimum acceptable standard, the more important aim is to consider how to move that practice toward the extreme of meaning and equity, regardless of the current position.

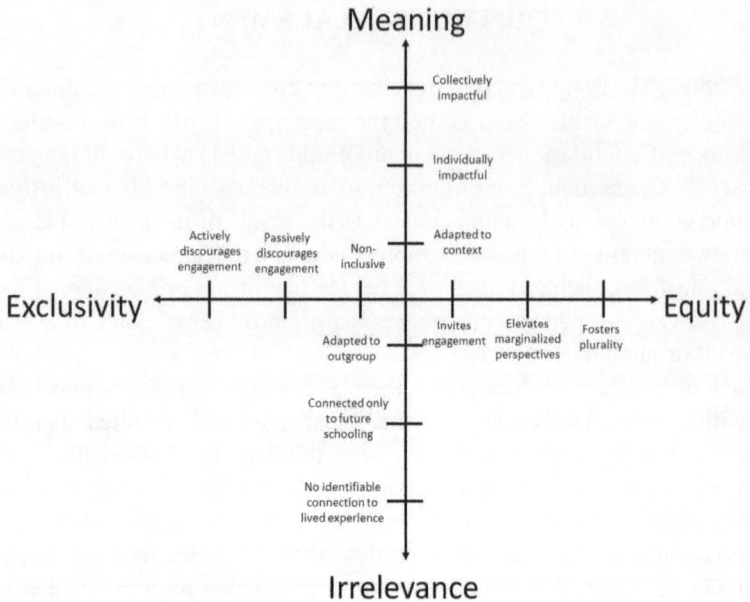

Figure 6.1 **Emplacement plane diagram.**

In the emplacement plane, meaning and equity represent the two axes with irrelevance and exclusivity as their respective antonyms. Moving away from the central point in each direction are incremental steps toward the extremes. These steps are essential in recognizing that meaning and equity are not categorical, but that a curriculum or practice can tend toward or away from an extreme. Ultimately, the aim is to place a curriculum or practice on the plane, not for purposes of evaluation, but to recognize what the incremental steps toward equity and meaning might be.

From the origin, moving toward the extreme of equity is the increment "invites engagement." At this point, practices and curricula explicitly invite all students to be contributors to the learning experience, rather than recipients. To move closer to equity, teaching must not only invite all students to engage, but must actively seek to elevate marginalized perspectives. This teaching does not simply let student voices exist, but attempts to draw attention to the voices that might otherwise be drowned out. In extending beyond drawing attention to particular voices, teaching for equity in emplacement will seek to foster a plurality in which voices coexist.

Toward the other extreme of exclusivity, the first increment is teaching that is noninclusive. These are practices and curricula which allow for the consideration that not all students will, nor should, engage. In schools these are often opportunities open to a limited number of students. The next incremental movement toward exclusivity are practices that passively discourage engagement. This could be through not rewarding or even disincentivizing engagement whether it related to grades or other measures. Similarly, these could be practices in which abiding by the rules of schooling is weighted heavier than actual learning.

The final extreme toward exclusivity are practices which actively discourage engagement. Although it might seem antithetical to have teaching which actively discourages learning, but there are many cases in which an approach to teaching will actively communicate to students they do not belong in discussion around a particular topic. Consider as example the proverbial "weed out" courses in many postsecondary programs which exist not to prepare students to succeed in a discipline but rather to identify those that do not belong.

The second axis in the plane addresses meaning. The first incremental step toward meaning in emplacement are practices and curricula which are adapted or modified to fit a particular context. This could be the inclusion of local examples or modifications to make a curriculum fit locally important topics. The next increment from adapting practice to context is teaching which is individually impactful. This increment represents a movement adapting to make teaching relatable for students to teaching in a way that has value for students individually.

The final increment toward meaning is teaching that is collectively impactful. This is not the same as individually impactful for all students. Individually impactful teaching leads to students saying "this matters to me," but collectively impactful teaching leads to "this matters to us." It represents a transition from seeing a classroom as students on parallel individual journeys of learning to one in which students are working together as a community. Collectively impactful teaching carries an implication of an obligation to others in the school or community.

Along the axis toward the extreme of irrelevance, the first incremental step are practices which are adapted for an outgroup, or a group to which some or all students do not belong. In a classroom, this might be adapting instruction to focus on preparation to attend college although that is not a route all students will choose. Alternatively, a lesson might use sports as an outlet to explore a science topic. This might be appropriate for some students, but for others who have no interest or experience in sports it is not. If a student later joined the group to which the lesson is adapted it could become meaningful, but it is not at the moment of instruction.

The next incremental step toward irrelevance is teaching that is only connected to future schooling. It is purposeful here that the focus is on schooling, not education or learning. Although teaching to prepare students for future schooling might increase the likelihood of them being successful in that schooling, if those ultimate aims are not meaningful that teaching is really only progress toward an abstract goal to which students do not ascribe any real value.

The penultimate step toward irrelevance is teaching which has no identifiable connection to students' lived experience. This is teaching of ideas which only exist in the abstract and either have no connection to the experiences students have as they navigate the world or the connections are not apparent or sufficiently impactful to the students. It is important to note that this marker of irrelevance changes greatly depending on the lived experience of the particular students in a classroom.

In placing a teaching practice or curriculum on the plane, an important point to consider is not the intentions, but whether there is evidence of the particular impacts. The important question in moving toward meaning and justice is not whether a teacher intended for a lesson to elevate marginalized perspectives and be impactful, but if there is evidence that the students experienced those elements. These are not simple evaluations, but ones that require careful examination of the teaching as put into action in a particular classroom. Ultimately, to improve teaching knowing where instruction is starting provides the opportunity to see where it could go.

CONCLUSION

Ultimately, emplacement is a necessary and guaranteed element of teaching. Choosing to not be attentive or purposeful in emplacement is not an act of remaining neutral in instruction, but instead letting happenstance be the determining factor. This is also an element which must necessarily fall to the teacher. Curriculum writers and curriculum directors can help shape curricula to give teachers the best opportunity to foster meaning and equity in emplacement, but ultimately teachers are the ones which put curriculum into action in their classrooms.

REFLECTION QUESTIONS

1. Which aspects of emplacement in your own teaching do you feel tend toward meaning and equity? Are there ways to mirror these aspects more broadly in your teaching practice?
2. With what concepts, ideas, or words do you need to engage in mutual teaching with your students? How might class conversations change based on this mutual teaching?

3. For one of your teaching practices, lessons, or concepts: Where does this practice fall on the emplacement plane? What modifications could you make to move toward increased meaning and equity?

NOTES

1. Ludwig Wittgenstein, *Wittgenstein: The Philosophical Investigations*, trans. George Pitcher (Notre Dame, IN: University of Notre Dame Press, 1968).

2. Stanley Cavell, *The Senses of Walden* (New York: Viking Press, 1974).

3. Derek Gottlieb, *A Democratic Theory of Educational Credibility: From Test-Based Assessment to Interpersonal Responsibility* (New York: Routledge, 2020).

4. New York City Department of Education, "Unit 5 Transportation Explore," accessed October 26, 2022, https://infohub.nyced.org/docs/default-source/default -document-library/unit-5-transportation-explore.pdf., 31.

5. Edward W. Soja, *Seeking Spatial Justice* (Minneapolis, MN: University of Minnesota Press, 2010).

6. Edward W. Soja, *Postmodern Geographies: The Reassertion of Space in Critical Social Theory* (London: Verso, 2011).

7. Stanley Cavell, *The Senses of Walden*.

Chapter 7

Gestalts and Principles
of Expansive Place

"I cannot . . . believe . . . I made it," I have a student pant out to me through labored breaths. I try to think of a more sensitive reply, but eventually go with the honest response that I was also surprised. The student and I were standing on a summit reaching just over 12,000 feet in the Rocky Mountains as a part of a field course.

My doubt that the student would succeed did not have anything to do with her personally, but rather how truly worn out and miserable she looked the entire hike up. For hours I had expected to hear a faint request to turn around, but it never came. She had "one foot in front of the other"-ed herself all the way to the top.

Just moments after dragging herself up the trail, she was suddenly bounding around the blocky summit. She stared down at the glacier below, looked in bewilderment at the marmot scampering across the tundra, and gasped at the expanse of land before her. As her teacher, I could not have been happier.

What did surprise me in my own reaction as her teacher is that as I sat with the greatest science teaching manipulative ever, the Rocky Mountains, I did not say much of anything. She, and the other students, were so obviously getting to know the place in their own ways. I could not miss the parallels to when I first encountered this spot when I was their age.

As a science teacher I had often taught content, and even content I loved, but this experience was fundamentally different. I was not teaching them a topic, I was introducing them to a friend. More importantly, I could not help but think that this friend would be better off because of the introduction.

A challenge in forming, and even accepting, a new conceptual framework to an understanding of place and the relationship between place and education is that eventually the framework needs to be turned into actionable steps. Philosophical musing about the meaning of place may be intriguing, but ultimately it is the actual actions of educators in classrooms, both formal and otherwise, which will shape how place is understood and valued in future generations. To begin to unwind the applied educational practice, the first step is to recognize what the end goal actually is.

William Rankin argued for the limitations of thinking to improve under-standing of place only in terms of accuracy and precision.[1] The temptation for focusing on equipping students to know more about place is understand-able, but that perspective fails to account for the ever-changing information landscape in society. Even if an emphasis on teaching to allow students to know more about place may have limitations, there is an opportunity to allow students to know about place in more ways.

From this perspective, the central argument here is that educators of place should not focus only on making place better understood, but also on mak-ing place better: full stop. Teaching for place that matters is not teaching that leads just to students knowing more, but ideally which aims to make the place more in and of itself. The outcome for this teaching cannot be measured only in terms of test scores, but must be considered fully relative to the improve-ments it offers to place over the long-term. Teachers of place are not trainers, they are social engineers.

The need for identifying outcomes in putting a conceptual lens into action is well illustrated by the 1971 Norwegian anti-expedition to Gaurishankar, a spiritually significant peak in the Himalaya of Nepal led by Arne Naess.[2] Naess and his partners wished to challenge philosophy of climbing expedi-tions, particularly on unclimbed peaks such as Gaurishankar, where the only limit on when and where to climb were determined by physical abilities. Rather, they wished to not only explore the peak, but embody a spirit of respect for the peak and the locals who lived near it and believed it to be spiritually significant.

The climbing team clearly identified what they did *not* wish to do, attempt to summit the mountain without consideration of local values. However, they still had to identify what they did want to accomplish. They decided to create a simple film for the trip highlighting the peak as well as the importance of approaching the mountain with an attitude of respect. In deciding that sum-miting would be disrespectful, the team did need to set an end point. The climbers consulted with local leaders who eventually pointed to a spot on the mountain and gave the climbers what they needed: an identifiable outcome that encompassed and represented their values.

GESTALTS

For educators of place, there is a pressing need for a metaphorical point on the mountain, a recognizable aim which represents the goals and values of the those engaged in the effort. Rather appropriately, it is the work of one of those Norse climbers, Arne Naess, that provides such an aim. Arne Naess is noted for his foundational philosophy work in deep ecology.[3] In gazing toward the metaphorical mountain of that work, the educator of place can start to identify the boundaries of that critical outcome.

A key element in Naess's work in deep ecology is challenging the view of humans as a being *"placed in* an environment."[4] As discussed previously, places are described largely by subjective characteristics which rely on a human to interpret. Naess explains this with what he terms *duplication theory*. According to duplication theory, the place exists as an objective physical landscape, with plants, soil, rocks, and animals which all physically exist. However, the place also exists in the mind of the viewer through the interpretation process described.

The challenging point with duplication theory is that the place in the mind is the only version which humans experience. If the viewer sees a landscape as harsh and inhospitable, that is what it is. A different viewer might see the landscape as wild and inspiring. The critical point is that this is not simply a matter of different perspectives, but rather that the landscape is something fundamentally different to each viewer. It is a difference of ontology. Each of these versions, the human and the place together, to use Naess's term, represent a *gestalt*.

A gestalt represents a whole greater than its sum, and more importantly a whole which cannot be separated. The place, whether inhospitable or inspiring, cannot be separated from the viewer as that is who gives the place a particular meaning. Similarly, the viewer cannot be separated from the place as the place is what gives the viewer the opportunity to experience and express curiosity, aversion, or whatever other values and emotions. Person and place are not separate components of a system, they are interwoven elements of the gestalt.

EXPANSION OF PLACE

In continuing the example of the landscape which is both harsh and wild, neither version of the place is right or wrong, but rather they coexist in a plurality. The place *is* both at the same time. The second version, wild and inspiring, did not exist until that viewer was exposed to place. Essentially, in introducing the second viewer to the place and that viewer forming a new gestalt the place became more things.

In increasing the total number and richness of gestalts which include a particular place, the place quite literally becomes more. There are more possible meanings and interpretations to which viewers can ascribe. Instead of allowing more people to better understand one single interpretation of place, truly allowing more people to experience a place in a meaningful way allows the place itself to become more. The potential for educating toward this aim is not a consolidation and clarification of understanding of place, but an expansion of what it is.

Teaching for an expansion of place provides a clear contrast to the continued compression of place in most current educational practices. Place is often relegated to a limited number of content areas and even fewer topics within those content areas. The push toward standardization has accelerated this compression. This compression ultimately makes place less than what it could be because it prevents many would be gestalts from ever existing.

The dichotomy of teaching for the compression or expansion of place might seem rather rigid, but the reality is that all teaching either makes the places in which it occurs more or less. It either provides opportunities for and invites students to engage and make sense of the place around them, or it does not. In so doing, teaching either expands the total number and richness of gestalts that exist, or it allows that number to remain stagnant.

The ultimate aim in teaching for the expansion of place is to increase the total number and richness of gestalts. This represents a departure from how objectives and outcomes in education are typically conceived. Rather than an objective in which individual students demonstrate particular skills or knowledge, this is an aim that looks at what students, classes, and even entire schools can tribute to the social product of place. Teaching for the expansion of place requires a different set of curricular tools and mindset, particularly in a society which emphasizes individualism.

In shifting from a conceptual consideration of what it means to teach to make a place more to the actual actions of teaching it is necessary to identify key principles which will serve as key points in the second half of this book. These principles can serve as guides in planning instruction or to evaluate current practices and curricula. These principles are not absolute laws of the only ways in which teaching can lead to the expansion of place, but instead serve more as search images for what it looks to teach for the expansion of place.

PRINCIPLES OF EXPANSIVE PLACE

In teaching for the expansion of place, there are four principles which lead to an increase in the total number and richness of gestalts:

- Expose more students to place
- Expose students to more places
- Expose students to place in more contexts

• Expose students to more perspectives of place.

Although each of these principles will be discussed at depth later in the book, there are themes worth considering at this point. First, although an obvious goal in increasing the number of gestalts is allowing more students the opportunity to engage with place, the focus is not based on a one-gestalt-per-student checkbox formula. Rather, there are opportunities for individual students to consider, appreciate, and even hold multiple interpretations of a place simultaneously. This means that teaching for place is never finished.

Additionally, to truly aim for the expansion of place, this sort of teaching cannot be relegated to a corner or carved out only for special occasions. It is not an addition or supplement, but rather a lens that should be applied across all educational practice. These principles are also not only for teaching that specifically targets place as a topic or for content areas which seem most closely linked to place. They are for all teaching.

CONCLUSION

In transitioning to the second half of the book, the goal is to focus on exploring pedagogical and curricular practices which lead to an expansion of place. Educators should not approach this work with any guilt about what they have and have not included in their classroom in the past. Similarly, educators should also not look to classify their practices as categorically good or bad. Although a particular teaching practice might be categorically expansive or compressive of place, educators are not. The true opportunities lie in identifying occasions to include more teaching for the expansion of place in an educator's practice.

A second important consideration in approaching the second half of the book is to not focus on identifying courses, content areas, geographic settings, or grades in which the opportunities to teach for the expansion of place seem plentiful. Certainly, there are settings which seem ideal for educators of place such as schools with extensive grounds, those located in areas with great biodiversity, or even those that have truly unique settings such as zoos.

Similarly, some educators might see particular courses as a great opportunity for the teaching of place, such as environmental science, social studies, or agriculture. Specialized opportunities such as courses based around student travel seem even more enticing. Although some of these courses do have ample opportunity, they are not the ones that give most educators the best opportunity to teach for the expansion of place. Unequivocally, the courses which provide educators the most opportunity to teach for the expansion of place are those which they already teach.

In the same vein, the students whom educators should seek to reach are those who are already in their classrooms. There are many schools, such as those in many indigenous communities or those in areas which are very reliant on agriculture, in which there is an obvious, urgent need to engage particular students in exploring place. However, the obviousness of those needs does not mean that a student who lives in the suburbs does not need the same opportunities to engage with place.

Instead of hoping for ideal situations, educators should adopt the mindset from *The Old Man and the Sea*: "Now is no time to think of what you do not have. Think of what you can do with what there is."[5] Educators must start from where they are and what they already teach and look for opportunities there. They can adjust planning for future instruction, use this lens to reflect on current practices, or ideally both. Either way, the question educators must ask themselves is, "How do I use my practice as an educator to make place more?"

REFLECTION QUESTIONS

1. With what places do you feel you have a well-formed gestalt? What experiences have shaped that formation?
2. Which experiences that influenced your own connection to a place could you replicate in your classroom?
3. In what specific courses, topics, or settings that you teach do you see the greatest opportunity to expand your incorporation of place?

NOTES

1. William Rankin, *After the Map: Cartography, Navigation, and the Transformation of Territory in the Twentieth Century* (Chicago, IL: University of Chicago Press, 2018).
2. Bob Henderson, "The Story of the Mountaineering Anti-Expedition of 1971," Adventure Uncovered, September 9, 2021, https://adventureuncovered.com/stories/the-story-of-the-mountaineering-anti-expedition-of-1971/.
3. Arne Naess, *Ecology, Community and Lifestyle*, trans. David Rothenberg (Cambridge, UK: Cambridge University Press, 1990).
4. Arne Naess, *Ecology of Wisdom*, trans. Alan Drengson and Bill Devall (London: Penguin Classics, 2016).
5. Ernest Hemingway, *The Old Man and the Sea*, introductio by Seán Hemingway (New York: Scribner, 2022).

Chapter 8

Pedagogy of Place and Transformative Teaching

In many ways, although place is a deeply complex topic, the challenges in translating that topic into educational practice are quite similar to the challenges in creating meaningful learning experiences for any topic. Teaching for the expansion of place is, at its most foundational level, still teaching. Practices and approaches which are ineffective or, worse yet, mis-educative with more distinct content will be even more so in trying to allow students to grasp the depth of meaning of engaging with place.

To start to identify and evaluate teaching practices toward the expansion of place, it is first necessary to develop a pedagogy of place.[1] A pedagogy of place is broadly focused on the "how" of teaching for place. This differs from different approaches to lesson planning or instructional design. If the focus shifts too quickly to approaches for individual lessons it can become tempting to identify one singular approach as the best.[2] Ultimately, teaching for the expansion of place is not a single educational objective in one course, but a theme that should be woven throughout a student's entire educational experience.

There is an artistry present in the work of educators of place.[3] Elliot Eisner defined artistry as, " . . . a form of practice informed by the imagination that employs technique to select and organize expressive qualities to achieve ends that are aesthetically satisfying."[4] That is to say in the teaching of place, educators are practicing a craft and ultimately a craft in which they reveal values and characteristics of themselves. Thinking of this work as an artistic craft requires educators to fully commit to that work.

Conversations around teaching practice tend to narrow very quickly on effective and efficient ways to pass particular knowledge to students or help them develop specific skills. For sake of metaphor, it is the equivalent of trying to learn how to play the first introduction riff of "Tears in Heaven" on guitar. If someone has no musical background and only wishes to know those few bars of a song to impress friends at social events, it is hardly necessary to study musical theory, chord structure, or even the names of the notes. "Pluck the bottom string without pushing on it, then again while pushing on the second fret, then the second string . . . " is enough.

However, if someone wanted to be a truly great guitarist, all of those other elements become essential. Questions such as "How are chords constructed?," "How do a guitar body and strings resonate?," and "Exactly how do I move my fingers across the strings?" are critical. Also, the focus becomes not one a single riff, nor even a single song, but how the instrument responds across a wide range of playing styles and uses. Certainly, the first version is easier, but undoubtedly the latter is more fulfilling.

As educators, there is a temptation to take the instructional equivalent approach of just learning a single riff. That can look like focusing on one particular approach, or just having a lesson plan which appears engaging in case the educator is evaluated by an administrator. Moreover, in the social media age, this is even more the case as the true nuance and depth of teaching practice is rarely made visible, but single images or a pithy quote about teaching can create the appearance of impactful teaching practice without having to necessarily deliver on that promise.

Asking educators to engage in exploring and developing a pedagogy of place is certainly a heavy lift. Teachers, whether in formal schools or otherwise, all face increasing responsibilities and dwindling resources. However, as Theodore Roosevelt[5] suggested, "Far and away the best prize that life offers is the chance to work hard at work worth doing." Truly engaging in practicing this craft toward the ultimate aim of expanding what place is in a school, community, nation, or even globally is certainly "work worth doing."

TRANSFORMATIVE EXPERIENCE

In developing a pedagogy of place, it is beneficial to start with the lens of John Dewey's theory of experience.[6] His central argument was that the experiences which matter in education are those which lead to further meaningful experiences. Experiences in education are not an addition, rather, Dewey argued that all students have experiences in schools. However, the problem is that some or even many of these experiences can be mis-educative in that they dissuade further experiences.

Dewey admitted the shift to the focus on experience is much more complex than an approach where content and standards of behavior are "imposed" on students. A focus on experience requires a number of considerations. First of all, there are implications related to assessment in that identifying an experience as educational in that it promotes further experiences requires a longer timeline than simply asking a student to demonstrate an ability to recall particular information. Furthermore, the relationship between teacher and student is fundamentally different in this focus.

In focusing on experience, teachers and students must work collaboratively where teachers attempt to create a setting in which an educative experience will occur, but students are ultimately the ones who engage in that experience. Beyond that, teachers and students must be in dialogue as to allow teachers to more clearly understand the prior experiences and backgrounds of their students to target designing instruction specifically for them. Similarly, students need to listen to understand the level of engagement expected and differentiate that type of participation from the simple compliance required in other classrooms.

In aiming for creating educative experiences, what teachers should ultimately desire is for students to gain knowledge and skills which they are then able to apply in other contexts, particularly contexts outside of the school itself. Transformative experiences such as these, according to Kevin Pugh, are those in which students show motivated use, expansion of perception, and experiential value.[7] These three aspects serve as a rather powerful guide in creating a pedagogy of place.

Motivated use refers to students using learning from a school setting in ways and settings in which they are not required to do so. Applied to place, this could mean a student taking knowledge from an investigation about local native plants and then looking for those plants in their own backyard even if not required to do so for an assignment. Similarly, a student could use their knowledge of local plants to suggest to their parents that they should plant native plants in a flower bed instead of ornamentals which will require greater upkeep.

Expansion of perception is related very closely to motivated use. However, instead of using new knowledge to prompt action, in expansion of perception students use new knowledge as a lens through which they view their daily lives. In this case, imagine a student who has explored how the water cycle exists in their local community. That student might start to then think of their own everyday actions, such as taking a shower, watering the lawn, or rain draining out of gutters as connected aspects of the water cycle, instead of detached individual actions.

Finally, in experiential value students appreciate new knowledge for how it changes their view of the world. As Pugh argued, "When students perceive the world in a new way, they often come to develop a greater appreciation and value for both the content and the aspects of the world it illuminates."[8] In continuing the example of a student who learned about the water cycle in their community, if that experience extended to considering the impact of runoff in causing erosion and transporting pollutants the student could come to appreciate that earth systems processes can be fascinating because those processes allow them to see connections in the world.

These elements of transformative experiences are obviously highly desirable in teaching for the expansion of place. Of course, educators want students to see how concepts apply outside of the classroom setting and ideally to consider and engage with those ideas when they are not required to do so. Obviously, educators want their teaching to allow students to see the world differently. Given the readily apparent value of these aims and the herculean amount of effort put into educating students everyday, a rather curious question emerges: Why are these types of experiences not the norm?

SETTING THE STAGE

The relative scarcity of transformative experiences among the myriad of formal and informal attempts at teaching everyday is not a result of educators not recognizing the potential value. Moreover, it is also not a result of most educators not desiring these types of experiences. Rather, the struggle is that these types of experiences require departing from much of the structure very common in teaching. The act of teaching tends to involve identifying a clear end point and structuring activities and instruction for students to reach that end point. However, transformative experiences are unlikely to fit this structure easily.

First among the reasons transformative experiences are unlikely to emerge from traditional educational structure is that they deal with an end point which cannot be clearly defined. Although an educator can desire for students to apply concepts in their daily lives and might even have some mental of image of what those applications could be, it is ultimately the student who decides if and how to make those applications. Those applications can certainly be recognized as a desired end point, but they cannot be clearly identified and predicted before teaching begins.

A second challenge the typical structure of teaching presents is that clearly planned lessons tend to only provide content and skills that contribute toward the objective. However, to allow students an opportunity to connect and apply learning requires offering a number of access points and perspectives not all of which will apply to all students or facilitate transformative experiences for them. Stated differently, teaching for transformative experiences necessitates inefficiencies.

Finally, the time scale of transformative experiences can be much different than the typical timeline of instruction and assessment in most lessons. A student might be exposed to experiences in which they learn the historical parenting techniques of Indigenous people who lived in their area. However, the experiential value of that experience may not truly emerge until those students are parents themselves and can appreciate the gravity of facing particular challenges with a toddler in tow.

Applied to a pedagogy of place, and in particular to teaching for the expansion of place, each of these challenges are extremely applicable. If an educator's goal is to engage their students in experiencing place in a way which empowers and equips those students to contribute to shaping what that place is and what it means, it is impossible for that educator to clearly identify that objective as it would reflect the teacher's values and interests and could be severely limiting for the students. The ultimate objective has to be identified *in vivo*.

The teacher's own experience and perceptions can also be very limiting in considering how students might use new knowledge as a way to view their daily lives. Considering the ontological differences in how each individual interprets place. What a school, community, or landscape is to the educator is not necessarily what it will be to the student. Planning explicitly for potential application of new knowledge then would be very challenging as an educator would tend toward planning those applications based on what the place is to them, which may not match what it is for students.

Finally, teaching for the expansion of place is very much a long-term endeavor. Communities and landscapes are not typically formed, or reformed, quickly. Participating in the shaping of place to create a more just, equitable, and sustainable world is not a skill a student can demonstrate on a quiz at the end of a school week. Rather, equipping students to engage with place is work that will ideally play out over a student's entire life. In many ways it is work that mirrors the quote about legacy in *Hamilton*: "It's planting seeds in a garden you never get to see."[9]

ACCEPTING THE CHARGE

The coming chapters will explore each of the principles of teaching for the expansion of place, however to accept the opportunity to engage in this work, there are a few realities the educators must accept. First, teaching toward this aim in inefficient. There will be efforts which will yield little returns and greater emotional, intellectual, and even physical effort invested than is strictly necessary to maintain employment as an educator. That is to say, engaging in this work requires selling out to the idea of teaching better, not easier.

Second, educators who wish to teach for the expansion of place must accept that much of their work will go unrecognized by current evaluation structures. There is not a standardized assessment that is able to detect students contributing to making their community a better place in some way. Although engaging learning experiences do absolutely lead to better content understanding, it is entirely plausible, if not likely, that any sort of value-added type evaluation structures will recognize the contribution of this teaching toward the betterment of communities or even society as a whole.

Finally, and perhaps most difficult, educators who wish to teach for the expansion of place must be willing to accept that they may never see most of the fruits of their labor. As students get older, move on, and disperse, educators may not have an opportunity to see if or how they continue to engage in place. Even if those students live their lives engaging with place thoughtfully and in a way that makes that place more welcoming and equitable, stories of those actions will in many cases never reach that educator.

These realities also pair with the fact, as is now often the case with most teaching, that this work will likely face opposition from some parents, the public as a whole, or even policymakers. There will be those that would wish for a focus only on teaching that translates immediately and directly to industry. Also, there will likely be those who oppose teaching with the aim of creating a more just version of place because they do not wish for equity as they are busy enjoying the benefits of their own privilege. However, none of these realities detract from this being work worth doing.

REFLECTION QUESTIONS

1. What transformative educational experiences have you had as a learner? What elements of this experience do you think made it so impactful?
2. How might you make instructional or curricular space for the inefficiencies of teaching for place? Are there particular topics or courses where you have more flexibility?
3. In what ways does your perception of place differ from your students? How might these differences impact experiences in your classroom?

NOTES

1. David M. Callejo-Pérez, Judith J. Slater, and Stephen M. Fain, *Pedagogy of Place: Seeing Space as Cultural Education*. Peter Lang Copyright AG, 2004.
2. Christy McConnell, Bradley Conrad, and P. Bruce Uhrmacher, *Lesson Planning with Purpose: Five Approaches to Curriculum Design* (New York: Teachers College Press, 2020).
3. Emily Christine Bretl, *Shifting Sands: The Art of Ecological Place-Based Education*. ProQuest Dissertations Publishing, 2020.

4. Elliot W. Eisner, *The Arts and the Creation of Mind* (New Haven, CT: Yale University Press, 2011), 49.

5. *The Key to Success in Life*. Theodore Roosevelt Birthplace National Historic Site.

6. John Dewey, *Experience and Education* (New York: Touchstone, 1997).

7. Kevin J. Pugh, *Transformative Science Education: Change How Your Students Experience the World* (New York: Teachers College Press, 2020).

8. Pugh, *Transformative Science Education*, 5.

9. New York Film Academy, "The Best 'Hamilton' Quotes," Student Resources, January 10, 2022, https://www.nyfa.edu/student-resources/hamilton-quotes/.

Chapter 9

Exposing More Students to Place

As children spend more time outside of the school day in structured activities such as sports, clubs, and academic groups, they are increasingly spending less time outdoors.[1] In teaching for the expansion of place, this means that contact between students and place that in previous generations would have taken place without prompting outside of the school day now requires intentional effort by educators to create.

More importantly, there are dramatic inequities in which students are able to experience place, especially natural areas. The reality is not that no students will be exposed to place, but that only particular individual students, typically those with some type of privilege, will. As a result, it has to be goal of educators seeking to promote the creation and expansion of place to expose all students to place, both local and distant.

INEQUITIES IN EXPOSURE TO PLACE

There are extreme disparities in exposure to place, particularly national parks and other public land natural areas, along racial lines. In 1992, only 1.5 percent of visitors reaching Grand Canyon National Park by car were African American.[2] A 2008–2009 survey indicated that proportion had only grown to 7 percent for the U.S. national park system as a whole.[3] In the same survey, white, non-Hispanic visitors accounted for 78 percent of individuals who entered national parks that year, despite only representing 63.7 percent of the U.S. population.

Although there are reasons to be concerned about exposure to places such as national parks for all students, it is particularly true for students of color. This evidence further supports the idea that which students are and are not exposed to place through opportunities outside of school is not a matter of random chance. To the contrary, this is another circumstance in which systemic injustices become apparent in the inequitable opportunities afforded students from marginalized populations.

There are a number of factors that contribute to the lack of connection between national parks and people of color. One factor that cannot be ignored was the specific banning of African Americans from state parks in southern states during the first half of the twentieth century.[4] Audrey and Frank Peterman also point, in part, to the lack of diversity in leadership in the national park system.[5] Joe Weber and Selima Sultana suggest the small number of national parks located near large population centers for minorities is a factor limiting visitation.[6]

Although individual educators will not be able to unwind these factors and other impacts of systemic racism on the opportunities for people of color, it is critical to understand their impact as it makes clear that the lack of exposure is not just a product of differences in levels of interest. Providing opportunities to engage with place only for students that already seem interested perpetuates inequalities. The takeaway point is clear; there are injustices related to opportunities to experience natural places and educators have an opportunity and responsibility to address those.

Not only is it critical to recognize disparities in opportunities to experience natural areas for how it might impact students of color entering the classroom, but also because the long-term sustainability of these places depends on the inspiring those students to action for their preservation. Stephen Lockhart, the Chairman of NatureBridge which connects youth in the San Francisco Bay area with outdoor experiences, argued, "We need to make sure these folks have a connection because those people of color are the ones who are going to decide whether we preserve public lands or destroy it for the natural resources it provides."[7]

As people of color become a larger proportion of the voting public in the United States, the long-term existence of public lands and natural areas requires that those places be places of value and connection for all Americans, regardless of race or ethnicity. As public lands rely on continued support and preservation from policymakers, or occasionally resistance from the populous when lands are threatened, the longevity of these places require a majority public support. In short, the current inequitable imbalance of users is not sustainable.

An additional area of concern in equity of opportunity for exposure to place and experiences in nature is for individuals with disabilities. Although this is a growing area of attention for the National Park Service in the United States, there is still need for concern. In many parks, only a small percentage of trails are wheelchair accessible and public transportation offered within parks may not be able to accommodate visitors with disabilities.[8]

Additionally, there are concerns related to access for individuals with disabilities that are not-mobility related. Although some parks have developed resources for those who are visually or hearing impaired, these are not necessarily widely available and can certainly impact some individuals with disabilities the opportunity to experience parks. As a result of the inequity in exposure to place outside of the classroom, it is critical that teachers create opportunities for exposure to place within classroom walls.

EXPOSING STUDENTS TO PLACE IN SCHOOLS

In focusing on exposing students to place towards the aim of expanding the meaning of place, it is useful to focus on two of the dimensions in Eisner's ecology of schooling: the intentional and the evaluative.[9] Although place certainly exists in the other three dimensions—curricular, pedagogical, and structural—focusing on the intentional and evaluative allows educators to focus on the purpose of exposing students to place. More importantly this allows for planning and evaluating instruction toward the goal of expanding place and not simply treating place as additional content.

Eisner wrote, "the intentional dimension deals with goals or aims that are formulated for the school or classroom."[10] In thinking about the goals or aims of exposing students to place in the classroom, there are two important points to emphasize. First, students need to have the experience of being exposed to place so they have the opportunity to interpret and develop their own understandings of those places, as Naess described.[11] This is going to require experiences where students are actively engaged and not just recipients of information about place.

Second, exposing students to place for purposes of making the place "more" requires having a goal of action as the outcome of the experience. Typical outcomes of retention measured through tests and quizzes are entirely inadequate, not only in assessing learning toward the expansion of place, but more realistically to even support planning instruction toward that aim.

Action as an outcome of students' experiences fits well into Eisner's evaluative dimension, which is the making of value judgements about what takes place in the school. Eisner argued this dimension reveals more than any other about what schools truly value. If students engaging in exploring and contributing to place is not a part of formal and informal evaluation there is a clear message that those elements are not valued as much as others. As such, in designing these experiences it is critical to consider the evaluative dimension.

FRAMEWORK FOR EXPOSURE TO PLACE

There are many approaches and strategies that could be used in designing experiences to expose students to place. The goal of the framework discussed here is not to be all-encompassing, but instead to assist educators in considering factors that will shape this experience for students. In considering each question, it is also important to consider that in many cases there might be multiple possible answers.

What Is the Topic or Standard?

With the wide range of content schools are accountable for addressing in classrooms, experiences focused only on teaching about the place are likely to always be fringe. Ensuring wide-reaching exposure to place in schools requires integrating place into the topics that are already taught. Additionally, it is important to think about using place as a route to exploring particular topics, even if the topics do not immediately or obviously correlate to place.

Although it can be relatively easy to imagine the importance of place within subjects such as history, biology, or earth science, the potential exists to integrate it in language arts, math, and art as well. This broader integration also allows students who are most successful or feel more confident in various subject areas to approach place using their strongest tools of inquiry. Additionally, with the trend toward more individualized plans of study for students, starting increasingly earlier in secondary education, exposure across broad subject areas ensures that all students have these opportunities, no matter which courses they take.

What Does This Topic or Standard Look Like in the Local Place?

The goal of considering what a topic looks like in the local place is twofold. First, this can be a critical step in looking for opportunities to connect the topic to place. However, this also opens space for providing the type of context around the topic that is critical, as Stanley Cavell argues, in creating meaning.[12] This is a similar type of application as seen in the push to connect content to occupational skills, such as integrating geometry to architecture or construction. This step in the reflection is also critical in helping design experiences for students within a particular school or classroom.

What Place Best Exemplifies This Topic or Standard?

There are particular places on earth that are particularly well suited to teaching particular concepts. Several American government topics would be much more easily taught in Washington, D.C., and Hawai'i would lend itself particularly well to teaching about volcanoes in a science class. In connecting students to place beyond the local, given the large amounts of technological resources available, it can be very helpful to imagine the ideal physical location for teaching a given concept and then allowing students to connect with that place through various media or remote methods.

How Will Students Interact With or Interpret the Place?

The balance of structure and freedom provided to students in interacting with a place can drastically alter their experience. The key point of emphasis is that it is ultimately a balance. Structure can provide direction and clarity, but does so at the potential risk of reducing creativity and expression. Freedom can allow students the opportunity to shape their exploration and experience as they see fit, but this freedom risks losing sight of intended topics and aims.

Not only is this balance that must be found for particular classrooms, in most cases it is a balance for individual students within a classroom as some students will need more or less structure. In considering the methods to provide structure or freedom for students it can be most helpful to think of it more as identifying a continuum and then adjusting for individual students' needs. The aim is to identify the ideal amount of structure for individual students to be successful engaging with the topic of place, not just to complete particular assignments or activities.

What Tools and Skills Do Students Need to Interact With or Interpret the Place?

Experiencing and interpreting a place whether directly or remotely is a process that requires a set of tools and skills. In particular, there are a number of technology skills that are essential, not the least of which is the ability to identify and locate resources related to a place. Additionally, many students will need to develop the ability to be observant and perceptive to not just retrieve information about a place, but to really experience it through the tools that are available, interpret it, and then communicate their perspective. The skills to explore place may not already exist for students who have limited prior exposure to place outside of the classroom.

What Action(s) Are Desired for Students to Take Based on the Experience?

To identify the desired action outcomes of an experience it is important to think broadly about what action related to a place can be. Of course, direct civic action, such as community service to clean a local park or writing a letter to the school board asking to have more native plants used in landscaping, certainly count. However, there are many other possible actions. Students might choose to act by communicating their experience or perspective in writing or through art.

The desired action could be, as Dewey described, a further exploration or questioning of the topic or even an application to students' own lives.[13] Regardless of what the action is, the goal is for students to *do*, not simply to know. From a perspective of planning instruction, this means striving to create transformative experiences in the classroom which invite students to extend and apply their learning outside of the school itself.

How Will These Actions Be Evaluated?

In evaluating the actions generated from these experiences, it is important to remember Eisner's explanation that evaluation is the process of recognizing what is of value. In this light, that does not mean that the actions have to be graded in the traditional sense. Teachers might choose to recognize the value of students' actions through dialogue with them about their work. Similarly, a teacher might invite community members or others outside the classroom to experience what the students have done.

It is also important to note that evaluating students' actions related to their experience of place could be separate from the evaluation of particular content involved. If students used a school garden to explore the math concept of area in choosing how many plants to plant, the evaluation of the action related to place could be the continued care for that plants, but the teacher might still choose to use another form of assessment to ensure all students are able to calculate area independently.

EXAMPLE EXPOSING MORE STUDENTS TO PLACE

In reviewing examples in this book, it is important to remember that these considerations of guiding questions are meant to guide lesson planning, but not necessarily be lesson plans themselves. This means teachers can use this framework and then build from their responses to fit whichever lesson planning model fits their preferences, needs, or district requirements. The

Table 9.1 Example guiding questions framework.

What is the topic or standard?	CCSS.ELA-LITERACY.W.5.3
	Write narratives to develop real or imagined experiences or events using effective technique, descriptive details, and clear event sequences. (Common Core State Standards Initiative, n.d.)
What does this topic look like in the local place?	Local creative writing groups
	Published stories written set in the local area
	Local newspaper
	Historical accounts from the community
	Conversations with local authors
What place best exemplifies this topic?	Dawson City, Yukon (Jack London *Call of the Wild*)
How will students interact with or interpret the place?	Use videos and photographs from the Klondike Gold Rush to document details (through drawing or writing) and compare with details in *Call of the Wild*
What tools and skills do students need to interact with or interpret the place?	Technology and ability to access photographs and videos of the Klondike Gold Rush
	Possible curated digital folder of materials if internet search is a concern
	Vocabulary appropriate to setting/topic
What action(s) are desired for students to take based on the experience?	Connect with a senior citizen in town to interview and then write a narrative story of an event from that individual's life
How will these actions be evaluated?	Narratives evaluated by teacher for the writing style, fluency, and detail
	Senior citizen provides feedback on how narrative captures and communicates their experience
	Narratives could be compiled into a book to have available at a local library

examples presented here are meant to show possibilities of items that could fall within category of each guiding question.

Example Fifth-Grade Language Arts

This example (table 9.1) is focused around a fifth-grade language arts standard focused on narrative writing. Through the use of place, the goal in this example is to help students understand that narrative writing can be a way to communicate experiences to others and help the reader imagine the experience even if they were not there. As a demonstration of narrative writing, this example used Jack London's *The Call of the Wild*. The text itself is a bit above a fifth-grade reading level, but excerpts or lower reading level adaptations are available.

The Call of the Wild is set around Dawson City, Yukon during the Klondike Gold Rush. After reading *The Call of the Wild*, students will use actual photographs and videos from Dawson City and the Klondike Gold Rush to compare descriptions and details in the book with the actual place. This comparison plays two critical roles. First, it helps students understand that these are real places and not just ideas from a book. Secondly, in viewing materials from the Klondike Gold Rush, students have the opportunity to understand the experiences that Jack London was trying to communicate through his writing.

In having a basis of comparison, students can consider whether or not the details of the book were successful in helping them as readers imagine what it would have been like to be in Dawson City during the Klondike Gold Rush. This also supports language arts learning as it allows space for students to consider writing and language as a communication tool. In this case, if the writing was successful, students will be able to picture the actual setting of the book.

To apply their understanding of how narrative writing can be used to share the details of experiences with others, students can be connected to senior citizens in their local community. The teacher can make the connections with a nearby senior center or assisted living facility. The student's job will be to interview a senior citizen about an event that occurred during their life and then use that information to construct a narrative based on the event. Ideally, these narratives would be shared publicly, perhaps by compiling in a book to be placed at the community library or even being shared online by having students record readings of their narratives.

Not only does the connection of writing narratives based on the experiences of a local senior citizen help form connections across generations within the community, it opens a number of other potential benefits. First, although the nature of the hardships will be different, many students will probably see some similarities and comparisons between members of their own communities and aspects of the narrative in *The Call of the Wild*, especially in more rural areas.

Additionally, the connection gives much greater meaning to the students' writing. Rather than writing just to satisfy their teachers' requirements, the students are now writing to share the story of a member of their community. Moreover, this can help students who might be new to the community to form new connections with those living around them. Ultimately students are contributing to expansion of their community by sharing the experiences of others.

CONCLUSION

As shown in the example experience, ultimately exposing more students to place through integration in existing content areas and topics not only allows the benefit of allowing all students to be exposed to place, but provides greater meaning to the content area instruction. This approach is not just about "sneaking place in," but leads to more engaged experiences for students within the subject itself.

Over the course of a school year, the goal should not be to look at topics and content for where it is obvious to integrate place, but rather to approach each topic or standard that is taught for how place could be incorporated. In taking inclusion of place as the default, many opportunities to create meaningful, engaging experiences for students will emerge. Furthermore, these experiences will better support students' subject area learning.

REFLECTION QUESTIONS

1. Which topics or standards do I currently teach that lend themselves well to incorporation of place?
2. Which of my students have had opportunities to experience place, both local and distant? Which of my students have not?
3. Is there a topic or standard I teach during the year that students are least engaged in, and is there a way to use place to make it more meaningful?
4. Which elements or individuals in my community are undervalued, and can I use a topic I teach to draw more attention to those?

NOTES

1. Richard Louv, *Last Child in the Woods* (Chapel Hill, NC: Algonquin Books, 2008).

2. Audrey Peterman and Frank Peterman, *Legacy on the Land: A Black Couple Discovers Our National Inheritance and Tells Why Every American Should Care* (Atlanta, GA: Earthwise Productions, 2009).

3. Nathan Rott, "Don't Care About National Parks? The Park Service Needs You To," NPR (March 9, 2016), https://www.npr.org/2016/03/09/463851006/dont-care -about-national-parks-the-park-service-needs-you-to.

4. William E. O'Brien and Ethan Carr, *Landscapes of Exclusion: State Parks and Jim Crow in the American South* (Amherst, MA: Library of American Landscape History, 2022).

5. Audrey Peterman and Frank Peterman, *Legacy on the Land*.

6. Joe Weber and Selima Sultana, "Why Do So Few Minority People Visit National Parks? Visitation and the Accessibility of 'America's Best Idea,'" *Annals of the Association of American Geographers 103*, no. 3 (May 2012): 437–64. https://doi.org/10.1080/00045608.2012.689240.

7. James Edward Mills, *The Adventure Gap: Changing the Face of the Outdoors* (Seattle, WA: Mountaineers Books, 2014).

8. Alexandra Charitan, "How the National Park Service Is Working to Make Sure All Sites and Monuments Are Accessible to All," Roadtrippers, April 26, 2019, https://roadtrippers.com/magazine/national-parks-accessibility/.

9. Elliot W. Eisner, *The Enlightened Eye* (Upper Saddle River, NJ: Prentice Hall, 1994).

10. Elliot Eisner, *The Enlightened Eye*, 73.

11. Arne Naess, *Ecology, Community and Lifestyle,* trans. David Rothenburg (Cambridge, UK: Cambridge University Press, 1990).

12. Stanley Cavell, *The Claim of Reason: Wittgenstein, Skepticism, Morality, and Tragedy* (New York: Oxford University Press, 2009).

13. John Dewey, *Experience and Education* (New York: Touchstone, 1997).

Chapter 10

Exposing Students to More Places

About seventy miles off the coast of Key West, Florida sets a small island which represents the land-based portion of Dry Tortugas National Park.[1] The island is the site of Fort Jefferson. As with many aspects of a fort located on such a small island with many miles of open ocean separating it from the main land, the sewer system for Fort Jefferson was uniquely designed. Although an unlikely parable, that sewer system ultimately provides a powerful example of the importance of teaching for more places.

After the outbreak of the Civil War, despite being quite far south, the partially completed Fort Jefferson remained under Union Control. As a Union fort, Army engineers designed the fort, including its sewer system. The vision of the system for the hexagonal fort is that sewage and waste would drain into the moat which surrounded the fort. The moat was held back by a wall which rose a few feet of above base sea level. Sewage would drain into the moat, the tide would rise, flood the moat, and the sewage would be washed out to sea.

Except, it did not. Sewage did in fact drain into the moat and the tides did rise. However, tides did not rise high enough to breach the moat wall. As a result, sewage sat in the moat and became a chronic source of disease for the soldiers and prisoners who inhabited Fort Jefferson. The design was itself not faulty if the tides had risen the amounts they did in the northern states in which the engineers were located. However, very near the Tropic of Cancer, the tides were much smaller. The design would have worked, but it would not work *there*.

Although a sewer system on a remote island might seem an odd analogy, it provides a powerful example for the need to expose students to more places. If a student is exposed to a concept related to only a single place, or worse yet, without any instructional intention to relate to place at all, it is entirely possible they might come to believe they understand the concept. When exposed to multiple places, it becomes apparent that they only understand the concept in that particular setting. "I understand this" and "I understand this, *here*" are powerfully different statements.

"I understand this, here" is a statement that implies that the knowledge is not generalizable. It is also a mindset that requires listening when considering a concept in a new geographical or cultural setting. That is not to say that some concepts might not be very similar across varied geographic settings. However, it is important to prepare students to not assume homogeneity as the default. In an increasingly globalized society, educators must not only prepare students with an awareness of the geographical diversity in the world, but also help them develop the skills to engage with and adapt their knowledge to those varied places.

In planning and designing instruction to expose students to more places there are two critical questions educators must ask themselves. The first question is, "To what types of places are students exposed (or not exposed) in this lesson/course/curriculum?" The second question is "What biases toward particular places or types of places are present in this lesson/course/curriculum?" Whereas the first question addresses intentional exposure to place, the second focuses on the implicit exposures.

As students are introduced to more places, whether through an opportunity to travel, or more likely through approaches such as photographs, video, and literature, they must process and interpret that place for themselves. If the exposures are educative experiences, as John Dewey defined, they ultimately lead to more gestalts forming as students are introduced to previously unknown places. Although the number of students any educator teaches at a given time is a fixed quantity, the number of possible places to which they can be exposed is practically limitless. As such, there are nearly infinite new gestalts which can be created in a classroom.

INTENTIONAL EXPOSURE TO TYPES OF PLACES

In considering the types of places to which students are exposed in instruction, it is necessary to consider the many continua along which diversity in place can be considered. First, there are opportunities to consider diversity in terms of continent, nation, or state. Additionally, places can be diverse in terms of their level of rurality or urbanity. Furthermore, places can display diversity in terms of geologic structure, climate, or levels of human alteration of ecosystems. Applied to social science topics, diversity of place may exist among types of government, cultural characteristics, or historical traits.

Not all topics and educational settings necessarily need to address diversity along all of these categories. In an earth science course, diversity in types of governments is probably not relevant, but diversity in geologic structure, climate, and location certainly are. Similarly, in discussing literature, the different geologic characteristics of the areas from which authors are located likely will not expand students understanding, but authors from locations around the globe, particularly from different historical and cultural contexts certainly will.

Intentional exposure ultimately involves educators making a choice to include particular places in their instruction. In many cases, this involves making choices to purposely include places which instructional materials such as textbooks or prepared curricula neglect. In a world history course, this could mean including exposure to more examples from the Global South to balance the typical Eurocentric emphasis or in an American Literature course that might involve expanding beyond authors located on the East Coast.[2]

This ultimately involves a shift in mindset for educators from considering particular places and examples as more important because they are typically included in teaching, to instead focus on elevating those places which are often excluded as those are the places to which students are unlikely to be exposed throughout the entire educational journey. The Holocaust receives large amounts of instructional time in most world history courses, as it should. However, this does not negate the need to introduce students to the genocides outside of Europe such as those in Cambodia, Rwanda, and Darfur.

Similarly, in a subject such as earth sciences that are typical classic examples of particular phenomena. Mount Saint Helens and Vesuvius are the classic volcano examples, and the 1906 San Francisco Earthquake is included in most curricula. However, volcanic eruptions in Indonesia and the 2010 Haiti Earthquake could just as easily allow students to explore the geologic concepts while also having the added benefit of allowing students to consider countries to which they likely will have very little exposure otherwise throughout their days in primary and secondary education.

It is understandable to see inclusion of more diverse places as opportunities which are great if educators do include them, but which may not cause harm if not. The reality is that educators do include messages about types of places in their teaching, whether intentional or not. Beyond looking for opportunities to intentionally include more places, educators must also look for the biases in their practice and materials toward particular places and types of places.

BIASES OF PLACE IN INSTRUCTION

There are a number of implicit biases related to place which can infiltrate teaching practices and curricula. In many ways, the nature and structure of these biases mirror that of other systemic biases such as those along lines of race and gender. The concern is not that teaching about the places which are privileged is necessarily ineffective or inaccurate, but rather than privileging particular types of places or even individual places comes at the expense of those who are marginalized.

The first type of implicit bias is that associated with the publication and creation of curricular materials. In most cases, textbooks and related materials are created by large publishers. These publishers tend to be located in metropolitan areas and also trend toward the coasts in the United States. As a result, authors and contributors for textbooks tend to be concentrated toward coastal metropolitan areas. A simple check for educators related to this bias is to look at the authors page of textbooks and see where is and is not represented among the authors.

In particular, few textbooks have authors from rural settings. Many textbook authors are associated with universities or publishers, both of which tend to be in metropolitan areas. Even if a textbook has authors from regions across the country, it is unlikely to have authors from rural settings. Additionally, these books are unlikely to have authors from other countries. Identifying these gaps will ultimately allow educators to start to identify particular places which they need to intentionally integrate into their practice.

A second type of implicit bias is that related to the personal preferences of educators. These can arise from an educator's prior experiences, personal background, or even just aesthetic preferences. For example, an educator who has lived most of their life in an urban area might tend only emphasize urban places within their classroom. Similarly, an educator from the western United States might neglect East Coast examples.

Neither of these are necessarily intentional, but are biases which can arise as the result of the educator's lens of experience. Those particular examples are what they imagine when they think of place and without intentional effort they could neglect to include places which are other than that which they imagine. Recognizing and acknowledging this bias is key to being to address its impact on teaching practice.

Educators' personal educational backgrounds can also lead to implicit biases related to place. A science teacher whose education dealt a lot with forest ecology could potentially exclude examples from prairies or deserts. Similarly, a literature teacher who primarily studied European literature might not include examples from other regions of the world. As with biases from personal experiences, addressing the limits of educational backgrounds requires educators to be mindful of their biases. Additionally, there is an opportunity for educators to expand their own experiences.

A final type of implicit bias which can impact curricula and teaching practices is local relevancy bias. This is perhaps the most threatening because in some ways it appears to be sound educational practice. Local relevancy bias involves targeting teaching toward topics or careers which seem locally relevant. However, this targeting can remove opportunities to consider places and experiences which exist outside of the immediate example. To consider the impact of local relevancy bias in action, consider an example of a school in a rural farm town in the Midwest.

Local relevancy bias might remove the inclusion of ocean habitats from curriculum to emphasize local agricultural soils. Although local agriculture might be a more accessible point for considering topics such as the water cycle, the exclusion of coastal environments removes the opportunity for students in that school to consider, experience, or investigate that environment. Although students from more privileged backgrounds might get the opportunity to travel to coastal environments, many students will not. Essentially, under the banner the of relevance in teaching, that school will decide for students that coastal environments are not for them.

Much of the local relevancy bias in curricula results from an emphasis on career preparation. In the example midwestern town, career preparation will likely focus on careers which students could likely pursue in the surrounding area. More than likely, this will include an emphasis on agriculture-related jobs, teaching, and healthcare. Interests such as art, literature, and technology might be excluded, and by extension, the places in which students could best engage with those interests. An exclusive emphasis on local careers might better serve industries in the area, but completely excludes many opportunities for students.

The reality is that implicit biases serve to limit students' opportunity to consider place only to the places with which the teacher is familiar or that the school deems relevant for career preparation. In this exclusion, the many possible gestalts which could have existed with the limitless other places are never created. Ultimately, those possible gestalts require educators preparing students to find new places with which they can engage.

Being able to identify potential new places with which to engage and then starting to investigate those places whether directly or remotely is a skill which educators can help students develop. To identify new places, students must be prepared with both the technological and intellectual skills necessary. Although these skills might relate to other academic skills taught in schools, in some ways they are quite different. In particular, identifying new places requires searching for an unknown, rather than an answer.

To teach these skills, educators must prepare students to not only locate information about place, but to consider the biases and perspectives inherent in particular sources. This is particularly true when using sources created by individuals not local to the place. Furthermore, teachers must prepare students to approach a new place holistically and consider a wide range of factors such as people groups past and present, climate, economics, flora, fauna, and many others.

FRAMEWORK FOR EXPOSURE TO MORE PLACES

As in the previous chapter, the aim of this framework is not to be universally applied across grade levels, content areas, and educational settings. Rather, the aim is to use this as a tool in identifying which places might be privileged within particular teaching practice and to then consider the opportunities for increasing the diversity of places to which students are exposed. Especially in an area where implicit bias can be impactful, using a reflective practice can make those biases visible.

What Is the Topic or Standard?

Most teaching for place must be integrated within existing topics and content areas. As previously discussed, content in all areas can and should be placed within physical settings. In aiming to expose students to a greater diversity of place, it can be beneficial to start from a topic which already carries some aspect of place. This could be environmental science content, social science topics, or topics that include elements of culture such as fine arts and literature. However, this is far from an exhaustive list of topics.

What Places Are Typically Used With This Topic?

Some topics carry rather obvious specific places which are used to teach, such as Mount Saint Helens to teach volcanoes, San Francisco for earthquakes, or Gettysburg for the impacts of the Civil War. In all likelihood, these are used often due to curricular tradition as well as the number of resources available. After identifying these typical locations, it is important for educators to consider exactly what makes them an ideal sample. With Mount Saint Helens and San Francisco, for example, it could be that the impacts on humans are very obvious to imagine and consider. This provides elements for which to look in other locations.

For topics that may not have a typical "classic" location used to teach it, the typical location may be the local community. This is often the case for topics like government. The local city, state, and even federal governments are not necessarily chosen because they are ideal examples, but instead because they are immediately accessible. When approaching a topic where the local is the default, exposure to a greater diversity of place allows students to not generalize the local elsewhere.

Are There Additional Places That Embody or Demonstrate This Topic Well?

For some topics and content areas identifying additional locations can be fairly obvious. Considering the examples of Mount Saint Helens and San Francisco, there are obviously numerous other places on earth with volcanoes and earthquakes. Some of these might even illustrate the particular concept better. With historical topics such as battles, there are battlefields and sites well beyond those typically included in curricula.

With other topics it can be helpful to phrase the question differently. Instead of asking if there are additional places, educators can assume there are multiple places as the default. The question then changes to "What does this topic look like elsewhere?" The question can be particularly powerful in designing lessons toward comparative opportunities with topics such as government, culture, or arts.

To What Places Might These Students Not Be Exposed Otherwise?

In some cases, a particular topic might be perfectly well addressed with an individual location, whether a classic example or the local. However, if the overall goal is to prepare students to be capable of engaging with place broadly, it is important to make sure that their education as a whole includes exposure to diverse places. For example, if a teacher knows that students have little exposure to places from the Global South across the entire educational experience, they should look for opportunities to integrate those places even if the content does not necessarily require it.

What Skills Do Students Need to Engage With More Diverse Places?

The skills necessary to engage with diverse places can vary widely depending on the topic and the prior experiences of students. Beyond the technical and academic skills, it is also important for teachers to consider the emotional skills that might be required. For some students, approaching a place different from that with which they are familiar is an experience they may have had through family travel and they could have been supported in developing those skills over time. For other students, this is an experience that could be overwhelming. As a result, the teacher must scaffold and support through that experience to allow them to be successful.

What Action(s) Are Desired for Students to Take Based on Their Exposure to More Diverse Places?

A critical element in considering the desired actions from students in engaging with diverse places is recognizing how this might depart from academic objectives. Similar to the tropey distinction between a tourist and a traveler, the aim in exposure to diverse places should not be for students to simply be entertained, but instead to do something with their new experiences. Furthermore, these are actions which should be immediate and identifiable and not left as vague future possibilities.

How Will These Actions Be Evaluated?

As in the previous chapter, evaluating the actions from exposure to diverse places does not necessarily equate to assigning a numerical grade. In many ways, the actions educators might desire from students in response to these experiences, such as giving greater way to other perspectives or considering topics through a more global lens, are very difficult to quantify and attempting to do so would likely cheapen the value of the action itself. Furthermore, evaluating the actions from exposure to more diverse places might occur over a different time scale than an individual lesson.

In many cases, exposure to a greater diversity of places is something which occurs over long periods of time, perhaps an entire school year. Even though an individual lesson might aim to create more exposures, the actions desired might not arise until those experiences accumulate. In this sense, evaluation might be separate in time from individual instruction or exposure to place.

EXAMPLE EXPOSURE TO MORE PLACES

In approaching this example, it is worth noting that as an agriculture lesson it does not fall under a broad national set of standards, such as Common Core or the Next Generation Science Standards. To remain a bit more generalizable, it is based on standards provided by the Future Farmers of America.[3] Also, as these are not officially adopted standards the grade-level application can be a bit variable, but this particular example is aimed at eighth grade. As the example includes the local as the typical place, the location for the example is a small community in Iowa.

Example Eighth-Grade Agriculture

This example (table 10.1) is designed for eighth grade around the topic of plant growth. In many cases, this is a topic that would likely typically only be approached considering local plants. This approach could be very engaging and might even allow students a number of hands-on opportunities to investigate the topic of plant growth. However, there is a great opportunity to use this topic to expose students to more diverse places.

A limiting factor in only using the local to explore plant growth is that although environmental factors and conditions can vary in a single place, there are limits to the range of that variability. The range of annual precipitation in an arid region does not come anywhere near representing the range globally. Similarly, variations in topography on the small scale can not match those found at a large scale. Furthermore, toward the goal of exposing students to a wide range of places across the entirety of their education, this topic represents a great opportunity.

Table 10.1 Example guiding questions framework.

What is the topic or standard?	PS.01.01. Determine the influence of environmental factors on plant growth.
What places are typically used with this topic?	Local community/farms
Are there additional places that embody or demonstrate this topic well?	Farming practices in other regions of the US Farming practices in other nations
To what places might these students not be exposed otherwise?	Indigenous Communities/Nations in US Southeast Asia Caribbean Nations Africa South America
What skills do students need to engage with more diverse places?	Technical ability to access photo, videos, and/or photospheres Observation skills in looking for factors affecting plant growth
What action(s) are desired for students to take based on their exposure to more diverse places?	Consider the impact of environmental factors on success growing crops in different locations
How will these actions be evaluated?	Through a written or verbal comparison of factors affecting the different locations Through observation of specificities in language use describing agriculture factors (i.e., "In areas with good top soil, plants need. . . ." instead of "All plants . . .")

Agriculture exists worldwide and as such there are examples from places which are typically marginalized in curricula which can be applied to this topic. Furthermore, as something that occurs globally, allowing students to explore this topic with diverse places makes it less likely that they will generalize the factors affecting plant growth locally across the entire globe. Essentially, it is an opportunity to make the "I understand it" versus "I understand it, here" distinction.

To exposure students to the diversity of factors affecting plant growth around the world, the teacher can have students use photos, videos, and photo spheres from Google Earth to look for evidence of factors affecting plant growth.[4] Although amount of precipitation and proximity to water are obvious factors, through observation other factors such as topography or human practices can become obvious. Furthermore, students can see how those factors lead to different agricultural decisions with what crops are grown.

A key distinction as students engage with the other three locations is that they are not looking for answers or "being told" from written resources. Instead, they are relying on actual observation of the place through media. This distinction is key as it allows students to engage with the place themselves instead of having it defined by someone else. Furthermore, this provides students opportunities to practice and develop the skills of engaging with place.

Each of the three locations beyond the local are obviously a departure from what might normally be discussed in this imaginary Iowa classroom. They also bring in opportunities to consider factors affecting plant growth which might be immediately visible in that community. This potential benefit to the content topic as well as an opportunity to integrate places which might otherwise be excluded from students' educational experiences make them an ideal fit.

The first additional location is Haiti. Agriculture in Haiti is drastically hindered by the dramatic erosion of topsoil, which is a result of the mountainous landscape, frequent precipitation, and French colonial-era clear cutting of trees to grow sugar cane.[5] Haiti is a country which often receives little attention in American classrooms, despite being located relatively close. It is also a location that challenges the amount of precipitation as the only factor affecting plant growth. With Haiti as an example, human practices and even economics suddenly become elements which can impact the growth of crops.

The second location to include is the Mekong Delta of Vietnam. Unlikely Haiti, Vietnam does typically make it into curricula, but often only with regards to the war. This exposure allows students to consider Vietnam as a place with distinct regions, and not just a war. The Mekong Delta is an incredible fertile rice producing region; however that production does still carry ecological and economic costs.[6] The Mekong Delta is also a region that has nearly twice the annual precipitation of Iowa, creating very different conditions for plant growth.

The final comparative region is Navajo Nation, which includes portions of Arizona, New Mexico, and Utah. Navajo Nation consists primarily of semiarid lands. Although there are ancestral agricultural practices which have been developed and used to still allow crops to grow, these farms can be impacted by mining pollution upstream.[7] Not only does Navajo Nation represent a departure in environmental conditions from Iowa, exploring this location prevents students from identifying a single "American" understanding of factors affecting crops to compare with Haiti and the Mekong Delta.

Ultimately, this activity is a rather small component which could be added to a lesson regarding plant growth, but it provides a very intentional opportunity for students to be exposed to and consider places different from their own. Furthermore, a consideration of factors affecting plant growth in each of these areas makes it clear that areas in which growing crops can be a struggle is the result of outside factors, not inadequate techniques. This is a realization which obviously can be very impactful of students' worldviews.

CONCLUSION

In considering the aim of exposing students to more places it is important to recognize the distinction between large-scale goals for education, such as students becoming responsible, informed citizens, and small-scale goals such as particular content. Although small-scale goals are important stepping stones, educators must invest intentional effort toward the large-scale goals as a whole. Especially in an increasingly globalized world, students must have not only an awareness of places different from their own, but an ability engage with those places and consider the experiences of those who live there.

With the explosion of distance learning, remote work, and social media, even a student who might live their entire life in a single community will interact with people from elsewhere. Moreover, their political and economic decisions will have impacts on others. In short, if the goal of educators is, at least in part, to prepare students to thrive in the world, exposure to a diversity of places is not optional.

REFLECTION QUESTIONS

1. What places do you tend to emphasize in your teaching practice and which do you neglect?

2. What opportunities do your students typically have to engage with diverse places, and what are the potential gaps in that exposure?
3. Which topics or courses that you teach lend themselves to an integration of more diverse examples of place?

NOTES

1. National Parks Service, "Garden Key," National Parks Service (U.S. Department of the Interior), accessed October 25, 2022, https://www.nps.gov/drto/planyourvisit/garden-key.htm.

2. Kris Fresonke, *West of Emerson: The Design of Manifest Destiny* (Berkeley, CA: University of California Press, 2003).

3. Future Farmers of America, "FFA Career Clusters," Future Farmers of America, accessed October 25, 2022, https://ffa.app.box.com/s/n6jfkamfof0spttqjvhddzolyevpo3qn/file/294160068843.

4. Matthew A. Clay, "Integrating Satellite Imagery and 360-Degree Photo Spheres to Teach Environmental Science Online for Elementary Students," in *Teaching and Learning Online Science for Elementary Grade Levels*, eds. Franklin S. Allaire and Jennifer E. Killham (Charlotte, NC: Information Age Publishing, Inc., 2022), 241–257.

5. Joel K. Bourne, "National Geographic: Haiti Soil," SOIL Haiti, September 30, 2008, https://www.oursoil.org/national-geographic-haiti-soil/.

6. Timothy Gorman, "Underdeveloping the Mekong? Extraction and Unequal Exchange in Vietnam," University of California Press (June 1, 2020), https://online.ucpress.edu/socdev/article-abstract/6/2/174/110491/Underdeveloping-the-Mekong-Extraction-and-Unequal.

7. Laurel Morales, "Navajo Nation Sees Farming Renaissance During Coronavirus Pandemic," NPR (July 28, 2020), https://www.npr.org/2020/07/28/895735482/navajo-nation-sees-farming-renaissance-during-coronavirus-pandemic.

Chapter 11

Exposing Students to Place in More Contexts

In the story of the preservation of place for what would become some of the national parks and forests in the American West there is a group of sometimes underappreciated heroes in the form of artists. The painters Thomas Moran and Albert Bierstadt, along with the photographer William Henry Jackson, played a key role in the codifying of the landscapes as worth saving.[1] Their paintings and photos were really the only way for most Americans in the east to experience these landscapes and lend their political support for their preservation.

These artists had a herculean task in trying to communicate the grandness of a landscape in their medium. Works such as *Grand Canyon of the Yellowstone* and *Estes Park, Long's Peak* both included some romantic interruptions by the artists to not only capture how these future national parks appeared, but also in some way how it felt to be in those landscapes. It is also interesting to note that with both of these works, the artists chose massive canvases at seven foot by twelve foot and five foot by eight foot, respectively.[23]

Even with amounts of canvas the size of small bedrooms and generational talent artists, these works still do not fully capture *all* that their respective places mean. The Indigenous people who occupied both areas are completely omitted. In fact, almost all human interaction with the place is excluded altogether. Similarly, there is no evidence for the adaptations that allow the flora and fauna of the landscapes to subsist. Nor is there much, if any indication of the dramatic geologic forces which shaped the landscapes to their current (at the time) form.

None of the things which the paintings do not capture are brought up as a critique. Fully addressing those aspects of place cannot be captured in single paintings. In fact, entire libraries and museums cannot fully capture the story of just one of those individual places. The reality is that no viewers of these work expect even these immensely talented artists to be able to capture all of these aspects in one work. The reason is, in perhaps the curricular understatement of the century, capturing all aspects of place at once is difficult.

THE CURRICULAR PARADOX OF PLACE

The idea that there are expansive topics in education which are difficult to capture in single works, lessons, units, or even courses is not unique to place. Of course, the logical strategy is to break those expansive topics into smaller, more digestible pieces. In many ways, this is what most approaches to teaching place claim to do. Geology, ecology, history, sociology, political science, and countless other disciplines attempt to carve off a single aspect of place and focus deeply on it. Even within these disciplines there are many subdisciplines which carve place into smaller and smaller pieces.

Unfortunately, what one is left with as they divide place into smaller and smaller pieces is something which is no longer actually place. The components do not and cannot actually exist in isolation. The politics of a place do not exist independent of climate, nor can the ecology be separated from the economics. All aspects of place are continually inseparable. Carving off a corner of place might be more intellectually approachable, but it is no longer place. Just as with the proverbial forest lost to the trees, the components of place together still cannot account for the whole.

The great curricular paradox of place is this: Place is too expansive to be fully understood as a whole, but also loses its meaning when divided into components. That means for students to understand place it must simultaneously be divided into components and left whole. This paradox means that educators must look beyond typical incremental approaches to teaching and instead look for ways that allow integration where aspects can be temporarily pulled out to be better understood but are never divorced from the full context which give them meaning.

CROSS-CURRICULAR LEARNING
AND INCREASED CONTEXTS

In pursuit of the goal of teaching for the expansion of place, to make place more, the first two principles explored dealt with increasing the number of total gestalts by creating more total connections between individual students and places. In exposing students to place in more contexts, the aim shifts to expanding the depth of those interactions. This is an aim which can even benefit students who have a reasonably deep existing exposure to place.

Whether exposure to place in more contexts results in individual students forming multiple gestalts or just increasing the richness of the individual gestalt is really inconsequential. The clear takeaway is that, as students experience place in multiple ways, what the place means to them expands. By extension, the place itself becomes more through the broadened sense-making of the students who are experiencing it differently.

Within school settings, exposure to place in more contexts typically requires cross-curricular instruction. Collaborating across content areas provides an opportunity for students to consider place beyond the silos of individual content areas. Additionally, cross-curricular integration opens up the possibility of increased instructional time being able to be dedicated to an exploration of place. Moving away from the silos of content areas to cross-curricular integration provides benefits beyond increased instructional time.

As students get older, even into postsecondary education, their knowledge becomes more and more specialized. For example, a student who is studying to be a geologist will focus their learning on topics related to earth science. Although they will gain specialized knowledge, they will practice their craft as a geologist in places which are full of many facets and nuances. Geology can be separated into its own in the classroom, but very much cannot in actual landscapes. Therefore, a geologist who is able to consider the full expansiveness of the many elements which make up place will not just be a more well-rounded citizen, they will be a better geologist.

As with other efforts of teaching for the expansion of the place, in considering which content areas to include in cross-curricular exposures to place, the goal should not be to only chose those which seem obvious. Instead, educators should accept as a default that all content areas can contribute to an understanding. The question to ask is not if, but *how*, a particular subject can contribute to an understanding of place.

FRAMEWORK FOR EXPOSING STUDENTS TO PLACE IN MORE CONTEXTS

Teaching to expose students to place in more contexts ultimately requires more negotiation than the prior two examples. Whereas teaching to expose more students to place and students to more places can be tied to a single academic objective, exposure to place in more contexts may not. Instead, exposure to place in more contexts will likely consist of multiple academic objectives, as well as some which might seem to be nonacademic. Additionally, exposure to place in more contexts very likely involves collaboration among multiple educators and/or community members.

Most educators, even those in generalist teaching positions, have areas of expertise that lean one direction or another. To truly expose students to place in multiple contexts then requires collaboration among a group of individuals with varied expertise. Even in a setting where an individual teacher may not have colleagues in a school with which to work toward such aims, they will likely need to rely on community members to broaden the total scope of experiences and knowledge in designing the exposure to place.

Furthermore, exposure to place in more contexts will likely represent a much larger time investment than a small addition of place-focused elements to existing curricula. In order to be good stewards of instructional time, teachers will want to be very intentional in planning these experiences to ensure that for the time invested there are educative returns in multiple forms. Essentially, educators will likely risk greater time and resources for exposure to place in more contexts and as a result will want to more confident that there will be a proportionate reward in the form of student learning and growth.

What Are the Topics or Standards?

The first point of negotiation in planning experiences to expose students to place in more contexts is that very likely there will be multiple topics and/ or standards involved. Even in settings where all subject areas are taught by the same teacher in the same classroom, each subject area will have its own standards. Instead of looking at an individual standard in one subject area for how it can be used as a lens to address place, teachers must fit together the puzzle pieces of multiple standards.

The finessing of multiple standards, topics, and subject areas also presents a unique logistical challenge. If the focus of teaching for place is in a single subject area, that integration can happen when and where that topic would normally in the curriculum. However, although multiple content areas have subjects which fit together and create opportunities for collaboration, it is very unlikely that those all happen to be reached at the same point in a school year. This means planning for exposure to place across multiple contexts needs planned far enough in advance to allow multiple teachers to rearrange their instructional sequence.

Beyond content area topics and standards, there are likely to be aims which might be considered nonacademic. In particular, exposure to place in more contexts will present a great opportunity for integration of social-emotional topics.[4] These opportunities are certainly worthwhile, but these objectives should be clearly identified and planned for from the beginning of the instructional design process.

With What Place(s) Do Students Need to Have Rich Experiences?

Although it is unlikely that there is any place to which students could be exposed and not absorb some benefits, there are limited opportunities to allow students to really understand individual place on a truly deep level and in multiple contexts. These are not places to which students are briefly exposed, but which they will know in a relational sense. To identify these places educators must ask, "With what places will rich experiences dramatical alter students' perspectives?"

One form these rich experiences can take are extended student travel opportunities. Over multiple days to even a couple weeks, students can interact with a place in ways that span multiple academic disciplines. In reality, an extended time in a place is necessarily interdisciplinary as the learning opportunities which prevent themselves hardly limit themselves to the confines of a single subject area. Even if the individual place is somewhere students never visit again, the benefits to a version of a case study in a place different from their own has lasting benefits for students.

Beyond concentrated experiences such as student travel, the places which are most likely to beneficial for students to explore deeply are those which have the most direct impacts on their lives. The most obvious of these is students' local community. Not only does the local community have a bearing on students lives, it is also the context in which students will have continued opportunity to consider concepts and topics. In addition to local communities, places which assert political, cultural, or technological influence over the local community could also be worthwhile for students to have repeat and diverse experiences.

What Are the Content Area and Non-Content Area Aims of This Experience?

Although aims are certainly related to the topics and standards to be addressed in an experience, they are not interchangeable. A key distinction is to determine within each content area if the aims of the experience are to introduce new concepts, reinforce them, or to allow students to make application of knowledge. If a concept is being introduced in one content through an experience there will likely need to be some explicit instruction related to the concept. However, if students are applying for a concept which they have already learned elsewhere, the teacher's role can potentially be more hands-off.

In negotiating the balance of aims of multiple subject areas, this potentially means that some areas will need more direct or intentional instruction time. Instead of allotting instructional time evenly between content areas, or worse yet by perceived importance of content areas, time should be divided as needed to meet the varied aims in each content area. Although difficult or impossible to perfectly determine, the division of time should be such as to allow students the best opportunity to truly and deeply understand the place.

The negotiation of aims must also include non-content area aims. These could have a social-emotional focus or might just contribute more broadly to students becoming informed, engaged citizens. The critical element to remember is that a choice to pursue one aim is a decision not to pursue another.[5] For example, emphasizing career-preparedness as an aim will come at the expense of subject areas or topics which cannot easily translate to a career. Although no experience can address all aims, the shortcoming is not making decisions which exclude the wrong aims, but rather educators who do not realize they are making the decision at all.

What Skills Are Needed for Each Content Area or Context?

A challenge in the negotiation it takes to create a cross-curricular experience with place is that not all students are fully confident with all the skills necessary to engage with place. In a single content area lesson, students having gaps in skills needed could cause struggle and might necessitate some just-in-time instruction. However, in a cross-curricular setting, students will likely have skills from other content areas. Instead of expressing their struggles with one facet of the lesson, they very well might just rely on other skills and ignore the area of struggle altogether.

A second aspect of skills necessary for engaging in cross-curricular learning experiences is that students will need to be able to combine skills from different disciplines. This could prove very difficult, especially in areas such as writing. Students might have written essays in language arts, history, and science quite successfully. However, combining all of those skills into a single writing project could prove a unique challenge as they seek to balance differences in tone, writing style, and structure.

How Will Different Content Areas or Contexts Be Weighted in This Experience?

A central point in the negotiation of a cross-curricular learning experience is determining how different content areas or contexts will be weighted in the experience. Schools, in general, tends to place the greatest weight on subjects which are assessed via standardized assessments.[6] However, the presence or absence of a state-provided test in a subject area is far from an adequate basis for deciding to weight a subject more heavily in creating experiences for students to engage with place.

Similarly, the characteristics or personalities of individual teachers should not be the determining factor. Perhaps a science teacher is the first to suggest a collaboration, but that does not mean that the most useful lenses in that experience for students to truly understand place are not historical or artistic. To truly engage in these negotiations, educators must step back from the lenses which have been most impactful for them to instead consider which contexts provide the best opportunities for students to engage with a particular place.

What Action(s) Are Desired for Students to Take Based on Their Exposure to Place in More Contexts?

In remembering the goals of transformative education, the actions desired from students based on the experience is not the same as the objectives or aims. If an overall goal of a student trip was to expand students' understanding of cultural diversity, what is it that educators want students to do with that knowledge? Similarly, if an experience focuses on the local community toward the goal of students having a greater appreciation of that community, what actions are desired steps?

A point in identifying the actions educators hope students take as a result of an experience is that although they do not have be quantifiable or grandiose, they do need to be concrete. Being "aware" of other cultures is not a concrete action, but taking advantage of future opportunities to learn about a different culture is. Valuing a community is vague, but volunteering for a community clean-up is not. Even if there are many possible actions that would be worthy, the desired outcome of the experience is action.

How Will These Actions Be Evaluated?

Evaluating the outcomes of an expansive learning experience can be very challenging. However, there are a number of considerations which can provide clarity. First of all, individual aims, objectives, and/or topics in an expansive experience can and likely should be evaluated separately. This provides more discrete points for evaluation instead of necessitating some all-encompassing grade. Also, multiple, focused points of evaluation make it clear how and where students are thriving or struggling.

A second point to consider in evaluation is that although each objective might have its own evaluation, there still needs to be collaboration among teachers in identifying characteristics of evaluation to allow students to demonstrate their learning as a cohesive product of whatever form. As with the proverbial horse designed by committee, a lack of communication between teachers could leave the final product an assortment of components to fulfill all of the checklists instead of something students deliberately assemble to represent their learning.

Finally, as with other elements of evaluating teaching for place, truly evaluating the impacts of expansive cross-curricular experiences with place will require looking past the items produced by students at the end of that experience. The impacts might be separated in time by months or even years. Although evidence of impacts for a student from an experience several months or years later may not be helpful in shaping instruction for that individual student, it certainly can inform practice as a whole toward the ultimate goal of making place more.

EXAMPLE EXPOSURE TO PLACE IN MORE CONTEXTS

This example (table 11.1), which mirrors elements of the Kids Teaching Flood Resilience project, consists of a project-based learning unit for high school which combines science, math, language arts, history, and visual arts.[7] The unit is for a coastal city which is frequently impacted by flooding due to rising sea levels, the physical structure of the city, and occasionally hurricanes. The goal is for students to create art displays which communicate the risks and impacts of flooding, as well as actions which can be taken to reduce or mitigate these risks and impacts. These displays will be featured in public places such as parks and school buildings.

To truly understand the causes and impacts of flooding, students must obviously explore the earth systems processes which are the mechanisms for sea level rise. However, historical engineering and urban design practices in the city will also have a dramatic impact and will cause the flooding impacts to be more dramatic than an area located nearby. Furthermore, mathematics provides a powerful tool in using quantitative analysis to consider the frequency and duration of floods.

In this project, language arts and visual arts serve as the skill areas for students to communicate their learning to the general audience. The authenticity of the task takes the focus from communicating for sake of fulfilling a teacher's requirements and instead places it on getting an important message to the community. The communication and analysis skills are distinct, but in the project work together harmoniously.

Although these elements work together toward the final product, it is important to separate the skills for purposes of evaluation. The emphasis for science and math is on data analysis, and a student could accomplish those quite well while falling well short of a finished product which communicated the results of that analysis well. Evaluation of such a broad product ultimately

Table 11.1 Example guiding questions framework.

What are the topics or standards?	Science: HS-ESS2–2. Analyze geoscience data to make the claim that one change to Earth's surface can create feedbacks that cause changes to other Earth systems.
	Math: CCSS.MATH.CONTENT.HSN.Q.A.2 Define appropriate quantities for the purpose of descriptive modeling.
	Language Arts: CCSS.ELA-LITERACY.W.11–12.3.C Use a variety of techniques to sequence events so that they build on one another to create a coherent whole and build toward a particular tone and outcome (e.g., a sense of mystery, suspense, growth, or resolution).
	History: HG.1.1.HS Identify and analyze the spatial distributions and patterns of human population using maps and geographic models and representations.
	Visual Arts: VA.CR AL.1.1 Apply organizational strategies that communicate a personal meaning, theme, idea, or concept.
With what place(s) do students need to have rich experiences?	Local community, particularly areas impacted by flooding
What are the content area and non-content area aims of this experience?	Understanding of the environmental factors leading to flooding
	Mathematical understanding of quantitative trends in predictive models
	Understanding of impact of the built environment on flooding
	Application of written and visual communication skills to communicating impacts of flooding with general public
What skills are needed for each content area or context?	Scientific and mathematical analysis skills
	Ability to access and interpret historical maps and photographs that show changes in the built environment
	Baseline language and visual arts skills that can be applied to this project

How will different content areas or contexts be weighted in this experience?	With an overall focus on communicating learning to the public, the communication aspects of this project will need to be weighted heavier in instructional time. Science, math, and history will be used to ensure the accuracy of the information.
What action(s) are desired for students to take based on their exposure to place in more contexts?	Beyond the academic aims, the primary action is increased civic engagement. Beyond public art displays, this could include communicating with elected officials or volunteering in community organizations.
How will these actions be evaluated?	Each academic content area will be evaluated individually based only on the standard for that subject area.
	Civic engagement will be evaluated by end-of-year student "exit interviews" where students will be asked about ways that have and have not engaged in their community.

requires teachers to consider the work carefully for what it reveals about the student's understanding.

Also, depending on prior experience students have had with data analysis, that aspect of the project may not need as much instructional time devoted to it. However, they may need a considerable time dedicated to learning and practicing the skills of using language arts and visual arts to communicate complex ideas. In the negotiation of instructional time this might seem like the math and science teachers are "giving up" time; however, in actuality they are investing time in non-content area skills which will ultimately allow students to make greater use of their math and science knowledge.

A final consideration is that with a project as expansive as this there are undoubtedly unforeseeable gaps in students' knowledge and skills which will emerge. This means that teachers must be adaptive and responsive to students' needs. Furthermore, all teachers involved must continue to work toward an overall goal of deepening students' understanding of place without becoming territorial or competitive about emphasizing their own content area.

Ultimately, larger-scale projects such as this represent an emphatic step forward. An individual teacher who commits to exposing students to place can through their actions say, "I wish for my students to engage with place." However, at the scale of a cross-curricular project a group of teacher says, "*We* wish for our students to engage with place." In that collaboration, place becomes not a point of emphasis for one teacher or a tack on to a curriculum, but instead a point of emphasis for a school.

CONCLUSION

In many ways, teaching toward the goal of exposing students to place in more contexts can seem like a daunting step toward complexity. The complexity might seem overwhelming, but the reality is that complexity is introduced because the teaching is gaining authenticity in how it presents place. Place is an immensely complex topic and although there are moments of clarity and some simple truths, that complexity is inescapable.

The reality is that increased complexity in the teaching of place means that what is being taught is actually place, and not a watered-down facsimile of place. Moreover, the complexity need not be hidden from students as to know truly know a place is to recognize that it is a complex, multifaceted entity. For students to know any individual place deeply, let alone the world as a whole, they must have the opportunity to see the co-existing, overlapping, and sometimes conflicting perspectives which make a place what it is.

REFLECTION QUESTIONS

1. Which perspectives of place might you tend to marginalize in your practice and who could help support you in creating opportunities in that area for your students?
2. In collaborating to create immersive experiences in place, which community members or colleagues are likely to be helpful partners?
3. What large-scale challenges impact your community which might best be addressed through a cross-curricular learning experience?

NOTES

1. Megan Kate Nelson, *Saving Yellowstone: Exploration and Preservation in Reconstruction America* (New York: Scribner, 2022).

2. Google Arts & Culture, "Grand Canyon of the Yellowstone—Thomas Moran," Google Arts and Culture (Google), accessed October 26, 2022, https://artsandculture .google.com/asset/grand-canyon-of-the-yellowstone-thomas-moran-1837-1926/ BgGVMnQig7OMJw?hl=en.

3. Denver Art Museum, "Estes Park, Longs Peak," Estes Park, Longs Peak, Denver Art Museum, accessed October 26, 2022, https://www.denverartmuseum.org/en/object/35.2008.

4. Christy McConnell, Bradley Conrad, and P. Bruce Uhrmacher, *Lesson Planning with Purpose: Five Approaches to Curriculum Design* (New York: Teachers College Press, 2020).

5. Elliot W. Eisner, *The Enlightened Eye* (New Jersey, OH: Prentice Hall, 1994).

6. Jack Schneider and Jennifer Berkshire, *Wolf at the Schoolhouse Door: The Dismantling of Public Education and the Future of School* (New York: New Press, 2020).

7. Mary Koester, "Kids Teaching Flood Resilience," Research Design, Teaching Practices, and STEAM Innovations, accessed October 26, 2022, https://www.kidsteachingfloodresilience.com/about.

Chapter 12

Exposing Students to More Perspectives of Place

A repeated theme in nature writing is the idea of an individual who goes into to the wilderness to learn something about themselves through learning about the place. The borderline trope is so widespread it can be found in works from the Bible to *Into the Wild*. Although often used, the idea is understandable. As illustrated in Naess's gestalt principle, the place not only reveals who people are, it *shapes* who they are.

The journey of sense-making in place is very long and complicated. The many factors that constitute the immenseness of a place are not easily, and certainly not quickly understood. Edward Abbey arrived at an understanding of place in the deserts of the American West not through small encounters, but decades of residence.[1] Simply finding one's sense of place is neither quick, nor easy. Unfortunately, neither is that sense of place one develops complete.

An individual's sense of place consisting of their interpretations, perceptions, and sense-making related to a place is the way they know the place to be. More importantly, that is the understanding of the place which guides their decision-making. However, that isolated "person in place" notion never actually exists. Rather, each individual's gestalts are laminated upon each other in a complex plurality.

Although there is a frequent temptation to conceive of place as being experienced individually, it is always experienced socially. Just as with public lands, all places, even if individually owned, are viewed and interpreted by many. As a result, a true understanding of place requires not only deciding what a place means for oneself, but also for others. By extension, preservation and conservation of place require not only valuing a place as the individual sees it, but also in all of the ways the collective sees it.

TEACHING FOR PLACE AS A PUBLIC GOOD

To approach teaching for place as a socially constructed and collectively held entity requires challenging what has become a central tenant of American education in the past forty years which is that education is a private good. Many of the attacks to undermine the public education system in the past few decades have argued prominently, and rather successfully, that education should be measured by how it benefits the individual.[2] That is to say that education *only* benefits those in the school or those directly associated with them. However, there is an alternative, which is to view education as a public good.

As a public good, education benefits everyone, both those who are and are not in schools. By leading to a more informed polis, and ideally greater civic involvement which comes as a result of education, entire communities benefit from schools. This of course requires a fundamentally different approach to how the success of schools is evaluated.[3] Specifically, this means that determining whether or not a school has been successful in teaching and preparing students to engage with place cannot be determined by traditional student assessment alone. Rather, it requires looking at the community and how it has or has not benefited.

Furthermore, viewing the teaching of place as a public good requires moving beyond, or, at the very least, supplementing traditional structures used in determining instructional objectives. Typical curricular scopes and sequences tend to focus on scaffolding academic skills that will allow students to be prepared for college and career. Career-preparedness is also incredibly prominent in how schools determine what is and is not relevant to teach. However, there are profound limitations to these as the only goals of teaching.

Although they are not typically listed as official objectives, and rarely, if ever, assessed, many teachers harbor implicit moral aims for their students.[4] These aims often center around preparing students to be upstanding and moral citizens. In many ways this seems like the most obvious goal for teaching and likely the best fit for John Dewey's claim that schools should do "What the best and wisest parent wants for his own child."[5] However, this shift in aims requires a dramatic step up in the aims of teaching from hoping that students will learn a particular academic skill to instead aim for students to make the community better.

Despite the attacks and shortcomings of evaluation measures, schools ultimately exist for the benefit of their communities. In many ways, schools are vital for preparing students to participate in a democratic society.[6] These are the democratic systems which Dewey claimed exist to lead to be a higher quality of experience for participants. Although this is certainly an intimidating scale upon which teachers can view their work, it is rather apparent that recognizing these grand aims and purpose should alter the nature and style of teaching practice for place.

TEACHING FOR PLACE AS A POLITICAL ACT

Considering teaching in general, and teaching for place specifically, as a political act seems to provide fuel for the fire of accusations of partisan indoctrination by teachers.[7] However, it is important to recognize that political does not necessarily mean partisan, as well as to consider what teaching as a political act in the broader sense actually means. This starts by recognizing that teaching is always political. Paulo Freire argued that education can never be a neutral act.[8] Education either forces students to conform to the world as is or equips them to change the systems in place. A third option does not exist.

When it comes to the teaching of place, teachers will either explicitly or implicitly endorse the place as is or provide the possibility of change. Moreover, they will either train their students to accept the place as it is, or empower and equip it to make them otherwise. In practice this means both preparing students to contribute to and provide voice in the creation and expansion of place, while also appreciating the voice and contribution of others. That is, teachers must teach for the democratic creation of place.

Teaching as a political act and critical approaches to teaching is not a lens which is unique to the topic of place. However, place does play a critical role in making all critical pedagogies more impactful. Freire argued, "Radical and liberating critical pedagogy must defend an educational practice where the rigorous teaching of content is never done in a cold, mechanical, or untruthfully neutral manner."[9] In this light, critical pedagogy *must* be sensitive to and engage students with place.

A perhaps difficult realization in teaching for place as a political act is that teachers must recognize that, if they are successful in their craft, the places they love and in which they live will change. The reality of socially constructed place is that places exist in the current form not despite the voices which have been suppressed and exclude, but because those voices are suppressed and excluded. Engaging students in contributing toward the creation of place means that their voices, and hopefully the voices they elevate along with theirs, will change the place.

Teaching for place is not about the preservation of place as is, no matter how much a teacher might love it. It is instead about creating an environment in which as a society a place is created to mean more and be more. This vision of equitable participation also means that teachers cannot only allow students to contribute to an understanding of place around the periphery, but must allow them to claim their role as full, equal participants in the creation of place.

FRAMEWORK FOR EXPOSING STUDENTS TO MORE PERSPECTIVES OF PLACE

Ultimately, teaching for place as a social project requires a different instructional lens. Specifically, the emphasis on place as a project, not product means that engagement with place can never be finished. Nor is place ever truly created as a final product, but instead is constantly in a state of recreation and reformation. As a result, planning for the teaching of place as a social project means departing from the traditional instructional arc of objective, instruction, and assessment.

In teaching to expose students to more perspectives of place toward the aim of more full participation in the creation of place, the role of the teacher has to be that of guide rather than imparter of knowledge. Direct, explicit instruction cannot facilitate a dialogue among the inhabitants of place and will likely privilege the perspective of the teacher over others. For these reasons, many of the traditional structures to designing instruction are not only likely to be ineffective in teaching to expose students to more perspectives of place, but might actually undermine the effort from the very beginning.

Teaching toward a democratic participation in the creation of place must be responsive to the needs and nature of the place itself. Instead of taking the place and molding it to fit a particular lesson plan model or assessment structure, educators need to reshape the structures and practices of teaching to match the needs of the place. Moreover, although instruction toward exposing students to more perspectives of place in one location can be a model for another, instruction which is truly responsive to the needs of a place cannot be standardized.

What Are the Topics or Standards?

Although academic standards tend to drive all instructional decisions, particular in primary and secondary schools, they may be counterproductive toward the aim of exposing students to more perspectives of place. That is not to say that academic content area standards cannot relate to this type of instruction, but they might be unnecessarily and undesirably restrictive. Content area standards do guide teachers in what to teach, but by the inverse property, they also guide teachers in what *not* to teach.

The reality is that content area standards start by placing particular topics off limits. Essentially, instead of engaging and exploring to find answers, in the broadest sense of the word, about place, content area standards can have the affect of only allowing students to find answers if they fall in particular areas. When applied to a social project of place this means that the recreation of place must still have particular predetermined characteristics.

Ultimately, the shortcoming of content area standards in teaching to expose students to more perspectives of place is that they are inherently undemocratic. They are not determined by the members of the community, but typically at the state agency or federal level in the United States. In short, although content area standards were probably not designed with malicious intent, they represent the values and interests of the state, but not necessarily an individual community.

With What Place(s) Do Students Need to Engage Socially?

In choosing a place with which students need to engage socially there are a number of factors to consider. First, are there places from which students feel excluded or undervalued? These are likely places with which students have contact and interaction, but do not have outlets for voice or expression. Alternatively, students might nominally have voice through something like a youth council or committee, but might feel as though their voice is not given weight by decisionmakers.

A second key factor is to consider the places which have an impact on the daily lives of students. Among these places could be school facilities themselves or public areas in the community such as parks or transportation routes. More importantly, these should be places which students share with others. The goal is not to segment a portion of place for students to have as their own, but instead to engage students in the creation and recreation of their place as a whole.

In What Directions Can Progress Be Made Related to This Place?

Civic engagement is a difficult and complex process. Although the efforts are certainly worthwhile, teachers serving in the role of mentor and guide need to help identify directions of progress that are likely to be made. This means that teachers need to consider the community members, decisionmakers, and/ or government bodies which are involved in particular directions of progress.

Furthermore, teachers must consider constraints in time and resources. For example, students with a couple months and few financial resources may not be able to make much progress in directions that fall under the purview of the state legislature, but could make progress with the local board of education.

This does not mean watering down students' ambition, but it does mean creating conditions in which students have a reasonable likelihood of being successful in making progress.

Whose Voices Are and Are Not Recognized or Appreciated Related to This Place?

In considering voices which are and are not recognized, appreciated, and given weight related to a particular place it is important to recognize the difference between nominal voice and meaningful voice. Nominal voices are those who are allowed to speak related to a place, but meaningful voices are those to whom others listen. Bureaucratic structures where opinions can be expressed is not enough if those voices are not able to actually impact what the place is and what it becomes.

A second factor to consider in discerning which voices are valued related to a place is the impact of token voice along categorical lines. Structures which treat groups of humans as monoliths without recognizing the diversity of values, perspectives, and visions of place which can exist in those groups. For educators this likely means looking for settings in which there is a categorical "youth" voice that does not appreciate the range of values which can exist among young people.

Finally, a critical point in getting students to engage in the social project of place means helping students recognize voices which are not being valued, even those beyond their own. Beyond that, the aim should be to empower and equip students to give space for these voices and to become advocates for more equitable participation in the creation of place. In short, students need to be able to recognize who is not at the metaphorical table.

What Action(s) Are Desired for Students to Take Based on Their Exposure to More Perspectives of Place?

For students to truly have ownership in the social project of place, teachers cannot, and should not, identify specific actions to serve as outcomes. However, there are actions which are likely to be necessary for successful social creation of place and which are important skills for students to develop. These could include how students engage with others, how they handle setbacks, and how they advocate for themselves.

An important point for teachers to consider is that although they may have actions such of these they hope to watch in students, there needs to be flexibility in *how* students demonstrate these skills. Furthermore, this list of actions must be flexible and responsive to the needs of students, the community, and the particular project or aim in which students are engaged. These actions must be thought of as instructional guideposts along a journey, instead of checkboxes.

How Will These Actions Be Evaluated?

In evaluating the actions involved in engaging in the social project of place it is important to recognize that evaluation must occur on multiple levels. First, is whether the particular aim to which students are engaging with place is successful. If students are aiming for a policy, design, or structural change related to a place, are they successful toward that end? This aspect of evaluation must be responsive to students' goals as the objective is to determine if students are successful toward an aim which they value, not one given to them by the teacher.

The second level of evaluation is focused on the process of engaging with place. Although students might ultimately be unsuccessful toward their goal, was the process they used to engage with place reasonable and appropriate based on their knowledge and skills? This level of evaluation is particularly important as it allows students to grow and learn from the experience, regardless of whether it is successful. More importantly, this evaluation can recognize and value that effort.

Finally, in recognizing the creation and recreation of place as an iterative process, a critical angle of evaluation must be considering if engagement in the social project of place within a particular context prompts further, future engagement with place. Ultimately, civic engagement is not something that is ever done, and evaluation of students' actions should recognize the continuation of engagement. Furthermore, this point of emphasis in evaluation makes clear to students that this is a unit or project focused on long-term engagement, not just within the time constraints of an individual course or assignment.

EXAMPLE EXPOSURE TO MORE PERSPECTIVES OF PLACE

Before considering an example of engaging students to more perspectives of place and attempting to empower them toward participating the social project of place, it is important to recognize that concepts and ideas from an example in one circumstance can be a model for another, but the lesson cannot be replicated elsewhere. Although that has been true to an extent for all examples in this book, it is especially the case here. Facilitating student ownership requires the teacher to not start with a predetermined direction for an experience.

The following example (table 12.1) deals with an urban school located in a neighborhood with a city park in disrepair. If the students identify improving this park as an aim which is important to them, teachers can help facilitate a project in which students seek to learn more about different perspectives in the community in order to prepare a submission for the city council requesting an investment to improve, repair, and update the park. This proposal

Table 12.1 Example guiding question framework.

What are the topics or standards?	Respecting and considering the needs and perspectives of others
With what place(s) do students need to engage socially?	Public places within the local community; renovation of a local park
In what directions can progress be made related to this place?	The teacher might feel students have a reasonable chance of making progress with the city council for a few reasons, which could include: • The city council has an existing public request process • The city budget includes funds for park maintenance and improvement • The publicity of a plan created by students engaging with their community and appearing before the city council would be politically difficult for the city council to reject
Whose voices are and are not recognized or appreciated related to this place?	The voices which could be privileged related to parks are those of more affluent individuals who have the resources and schedule flexibility to attend city council members. Voices which could be underappreciated are likely those of the students' themselves, recent immigrants who might be nervous to engage with a government agency, and low-income senior citizens in the community
What action(s) are desired for students to take based on their exposure to more perspectives of place?	Prepare and present an official proposal to the city council based on in-depth and broad community input

| How will these actions be evaluated? | Ideally, the action will be evaluated by whether students are able to get the city council to commit to renovating the park. However, there is also an opportunity to consider how they gather and consider diverse perspectives. In the long-term the aim is for students to continue to engage in civil processes. |

should use evidence and statements gathered from the community to make a compelling argument.

Identifying what the students themselves might want in the park is a relatively easy task. Perhaps this includes facilities such as a skate park, basketball court, or gathering places. However, to make a compelling case, the students will need to gather perspectives from around the community. This could involve planning listening sessions with different community members or creating and distributing a survey in the community. In collecting that information students will need to understand and consider the perspectives of others and help balance those into a proposal which will have broad support.

Working on a project for a public place within a community requires that students not only understand multiple diverse perspectives, but that they are able to balance those in a way which can help consensus within the community. Furthermore, as was discussed in the chapter related to public places, engaging with these types of places is a way for students to make their needs and values public. As young people become full civic participants, an opportunity to make *their* perspective visible is key.

CONCLUSION

Teaching to expose students to more perspectives of place and to engage in the social project of place can certainly be intimidating. This manner of teaching carries a complexity not found the more sanitized lessons which deal with a single concept and typically remove it from its context. However, these complexities are not a result of poor instructional planning, but the realities of being a member of a community. In other words, this is not complexity introduced by this manner of teaching, and instead is complexity from which students are not sheltered.

Much of teaching practice and instructional design tends to focus on preparing students for future education. The oft-used phrase "on grade leve" is indicative of this as it implies whether a student is on pace for some future education. Teaching to expose students to more perspectives of place does not settle for preparing students only for future education, but instead preparation for living and being a part of a society in particular communities. Although students will hopefully continue their education past any given point, it is not a guarantee. To the contrary, students are guaranteed to live in and belong to a community.

REFLECTION QUESTIONS

1. In what ways are your students' voices marginalized, and what opportunities might there be to engage them socially with place?
2. What are the greatest needs in your community? Are there way for students to work toward addressing at least part of these needs?
3. What skills do you need to develop as an educator to better mentor and support students participating in civic engagement in place?

NOTES

1. Edward Abbey, *Desert Solitaire* (New York: Touchstone, 1990).

2. Jack Schneider and Jennifer Berkshire, *Wolf at the Schoolhouse Door: The Dismantling of Public Education and the Future of School* (New York: The New Press, 2020).

3. Derek Gottlieb, *A Democratic Theory of Educational Credibility: From Test-Based Assessment to Interpersonal Responsibility* (New York: Routledge, 2020).

4. Matthew A. Clay, "Student Success on the High Plains of Western Kansas," *Curriculum and Teaching Dialogue 23*, no. 1 (2021): 7–20.

5. John Dewey, *The School and Society* (Chicago, IL: University of Chicago Press, 1968), 3.

6. Schneider and Berkshire, *Wolf at the Schoolhouse Door*.

7. Yue Stella Yu and Isabel Lohman, "Culture Wars Divide Michigan Schools: How Many Rights Should Parents Have?" *Bridge Michigan*, September 23, 2022, https://www.bridgemi.com/talent-education/culture-wars-divide-michigan-schools-how-many-rights-should-parents-have.

8. Paulo Freire, *Pedagogy of the Oppressed* (Harmondsworth, UK: Penguin Education, 1972).

9. Paulo Freire, *Pedagogy of Indignation* (London: Routledge, 2016), 19.

Chapter 13

Toward Landscapes of Justice

A question which, although critical, is not often asked is "toward what ends?" Teaching practices frequently change and innovations of teaching practice along particular lines of inquiry, but at times it is easy for educators to metaphorically keep their heads down in attempting to make progress and forget to look up to determine toward what that progress is being made. To ask educators to approach teaching for place in rather different manner necessitates providing a vision of a point on the horizon toward which this effort is progressing. In short, that point is a more just iteration of place.

As explored previously in this book, if place is created through social interactions and engagement and not inherent, that means it can be made to be other than it currently is. There are countless injustices related to place, such as disproportionate impacts of climate change experienced by people who are the most vulnerable, lack of access to parks and green spaces for those who are marginalized, and the minimization or exclusion of the voices of those from particular places. However, these unjust versions of place can be recreated in the direction of justice using social processes not all that different from those which led to the present version.

Justice is certainly a desirable goal for all facets of education, but it carries particular weight when discussed relative to place. Justice in academic achievement leads to equity in students' opportunity to engage with and understand concepts. Justice in place is a fundamental reshaping of the places where students are, where they exist. Moreover, in light of Naess's gestalt theory, justice in place creates equity in *who* students are and who they are allowed to be.

A challenge in looking for and pursuing justice in place is that place is never a finished product. A place as it exists today is not a completed version; rather it is a single frame from a very long movie. The question is not "is this place just?," rather it is "is this place just, at this moment?" Looking for and fostering justice in place is a cycle of constant evaluation and reevaluation.

The complexity and ambiguity are intimidating, but the possibility of justice embodied in a place as the potential reward makes this endeavor worthwhile.

SPECIES IN NEED OF CONSERVATION

Although justice in place is an admirable goal, and pretty firmly answers the question of "to what ends?," the mechanisms and steps for creating a more just place are certainly less than obvious. Providing a grandiose idea is relatively easy compared to the actionable steps it takes to move toward that goal. Furthermore, the specificity of place means that strategies in pursuit of justice in one place are not necessarily replicable elsewhere. Although there are not strategies which can be guaranteed to work in every setting to produce justice, there are threats which apply across most settings likely to prevent it.

Before discussing the threats and barriers to justice in place, it is first necessary to revisit the concept of gestalts. It can be tempting to consider gestalts as finished products, but as with place in general that is never the case. A gestalt is not formed in the sense of checking a box, but is grown and nurtured. Gestalts are not products; they are living organisms. As an individual gets to know a place more, better, or differently, the gestalt changes, expands, and grows. Ultimately, a landscape of justice is one in which all gestalts are unimpeded from forming and growing in many directions.

Gestalts are not only like living organisms in that they continue to grow and change over time, they also are similar to organisms in that they need protection and care. In the wildlife biology world these organisms are called Species in Need of Conservation (SINC).[1] SINC species are those which may require habitat preservation or protection, might need captive breeding programs to help maintain genetic diversity, or perhaps they also need special protections during particular times of the year such as mating seasons. Whatever the potential actions to help conserve the species, it is critical to understand why it is in need of conservation at all.

SINC species can face numerous threats. Many times, these are related to destruction of habitat, impacts of climate change, or competition with or predation by invasive species. In short, there is a reason that particular species needs help. Gestalts are not different. There are factors which threaten the opportunity for the formation or growth of gestalts. In identifying these threats, educators seeking to foster justice in place can have a clear vision for what they are up against.

Unfortunately, education broadly is not a cure-all to combat these threats. In fact, the education system was very much present for the processes which have led to unjust versions of place. Education has fostered the threats. To quote a 1970 Earth Day poster, "We have met the enemy and he is us."[2]

However, instead of bemoaning past failures, it is instead much more helpful to identify the ways in which education presently threatens the SINC species of gestalts.

THREATS TO GESTALTS

The first way in which education threatens the formation and propagation of gestalts is by attempting to not address place at all. Even though the discussion of implicit bias has shown that teaching always carries a message about place, there are many practices, policies, and curricula which attempt or claim to be placeless. These practices tend to use phrases such as "works in any school" and do not label themselves as placeless, but instead by the much more common phrase: standardized.

The push toward standardization is undoubtedly a threat to gestalts as a SINC species. Gestalts are highly personal. Standardized curricula and especially standardized assessments cannot account for the personal nature and variability of gestalts. Standardized education claims to be for anywhere, but in reality, is for nowhere. For gestalts to thrive requires education for the place in which it occurs, which is the antithesis of standardization.

A second way in which education poses a threat to gestalts is through the banking of particular interpretations of place. Beyond the shortcoming of banking place discussed in prior chapters, another threatening banked idea related to place is that school and community are separate and distinct. There are many ways in which this can occur but likely the most prevalent are the constant distinctions between school and the "real world." The phrasing and distinction send a very clear message that inside and outside of the school are separate places instead of both being components of a larger whole.

Beyond the ways in which the separation of school and community are banked in students, the same message is also banked in community members. When community members and parents are not invited into the school, other than when it benefits the school, it sends a clear message to the community that the school is an entity to which they do not belong and cannot contribute. Furthermore, many security measures put in place by schools, multiple locked doors with check-in systems, reinforce the message that the community and school are separate.

A final threat to gestalts that is education-related is the potential privatization of public education spaces. The privatization of education movement through programs such as vouchers is gaining steady momentum.[3] Although there are many implications to this movement, one which is not often discussed is that when a public school is privatized, lost, or consolidated, the surrounding community loses one of its primary public spaces. This is particularly true for rural communities where school buildings are civic and cultural centers. A place which can foster the growth of gestalts becomes metaphorically, or perhaps literally, gated off.

Many of the risks posed by movements to privatize public federal lands are also found in the potential privatization of schools. Instead of schools being public spaces where people, especially young people, can make their needs and values visible, private schools only allow that opportunity for those which they select. Furthermore, public schools have institutions of oversight such as boards of education and state legislatures which allow for public input, which may not be present in a privatized school.

Finally, the privatization of education presents another risk to the growth of gestalts because it codifies the belief that education is a public good. As discussed in the previous chapter, the social project of place can lead to richer, deeper gestalts. Privatization makes clear that schools should only be evaluated by how they benefit the individual student, and not for how it impacts the community. It is difficult to teach toward creating equity in a social project when the prevailing framework does not leave room for public goods.

Fortunately, there are ways for educators to combat all of these threats. They not only can intentionally include place in their teaching, but do so in a way that allows students to explore and engage with place for sense-making both individually and collectively. Additionally, educators can work to oppose the privatization of education through civic and political engagement. They can also continue to advocate for the maintenance of the public education system by reaching out to and connecting with community members.

THE SCOPE OF THE WORK

For educators to help move their communities toward being places of justice they must accept that impacting the community itself falls within the scope of not only the impact of their work, but also their capabilities. Especially in an area where teachers are often evaluated by metrics such as "value added" as determine by state assessment scores, it can be easy to narrowly define the scope of teachers' work by whether students do or do not learn particular content.[4] However, this greatly undersells the potential of what teachers can do.

The reality is that public education originally existed specifically to be a benefit to the local community. Furthermore, many prominent societal steps toward justice have come with some sort of large educational component, whether formal or informal. As Nelson Mandela argued, "Education is the most powerful weapon you can use to change the world."[5] Education can and has dramatically changed places.

There are many individuals who undersell the potential of educators, whether politicians, media, or the public at large. It is critical that teachers themselves do not join in this doubt. Furthermore, the ultimate rebuttal for those who claim that teachers cannot have an impact on a place or community as a whole is for teachers to demonstrably show that is not the case. Schools might tend to brag about test scores, college acceptance rates, or athletic success, but they also need to brag about how they have been able to positively impact their community.

CONCLUSION

A critical point about species in need of conservation is that, however concerning, the designation is not the same as a species which is extinct. A species which is extinct can only be spoken of in the past tense. The game is over and the species is gone. Famous more recent extinctions such as the passenger pigeon, Steller's sea cow, and great auk all represent what was. Certainly, more can be learned about all these species, but even with increased knowledge there is still not a future for them.

In contrast, species in need of conservation do have a future. Their future might be concerning and face many challenges and threats; however, a future does exist. By having a future as an option there is also the critical opportunity to make that future different than its current direction. Even if the current score is lopsided, the game is very much not over. Something can still be done.

In thinking of gestalts as a species in need of conservation, they also are very much not extinct. Even if a teacher has not previously tried to engage students with place, the opportunity still exists for a future in which those students do form a connection to place. The game is not over. Despite being surrounded by threats, teachers for place can still engage students in their local landscape and community. Teachers still have the opportunity to empower students to reshape those places. Not only do those places have a future they can have a future where place is more just.

Beyond realizing the possibility for teachers to better the communities in which they live, it is important to start considering that element in teacher evaluation. This could mean providing space for educators to share their successes and failures in engaging their students in the social project of place. Also, teachers must evaluate their own beliefs related to the ability to impact their community. In short, teachers cannot undersell their own value.

Although this work is complicated and overwhelming, the potential for schools to better their communities toward a more just version of place is very worthwhile. Many adults wish for their children to inherit a better version of the world. Instead of passively hoping, this mindset allows teachers to actively try to create the version of place in which they want to live and in which they want their students to grow up.

REFLECTION QUESTIONS

1. What specific threats exist in your school and community to students being able to engage with place?
2. What are the largest barriers to justice in your school and community? In what ways can you aim to address those as an educator?
3. How might you frame the scope of your work as an educator to the public to better allow them to understand the potential impact education can have?

NOTES

1. Edward O. Wilson, *Half-Earth: Our Planet's Fight for Life* (New York: Liveright Publishing Corporation, 2017).

2. Billy Ireland Cartoon Library and Museum, "We Have Met the Enemy and He Is Us,'" Tales from the Vault 40 Years 40 Stories, accessed October 26, 2022, https://library.osu.edu/site/40stories/2020/01/05/we-have-met-the-enemy/.

3. Jack Schneider and Jennifer Berkshire, *Wolf at the Schoolhouse Door: The Dismantling of Public Education and the Future of School* (New York: New Press, 2020).

4. Derek Gottlieb, *Education Reform and the Concept of Good Teaching* (New York: Routledge, 2015).

5. Punjab Colleges, "Education Is the Most Powerful Weapon," Punjab Colleges, accessed October 26, 2022, https://pgc.edu/education-is-the-most-powerful-weapon/#:~:text=%E2%80%9CEducation%20is%20the%20most%20powerful,about%20what%20happens%20around%20us.

Chapter 14

The Teacher Steward

To bring this framework for the role of education in the creation of place to a close it is critical to consider how this perspective reimagines the role of the teacher. A more expansive understanding of the connection between education and place necessitates an accompanying broader recognition of the role of teachers. Before diving into this role, it is first necessary to recognize that what is considered a teacher here might carry a great many professional job titles. Whether a school administrator, formal educator, or informal educator, all teachers have a role in the creation of place.

Additionally, it is critical to recognize that this is not an additional role for teachers who are by and large overworked and strained. Rather, this is an acknowledgment of the role these teachers are already serving in the creation of place. Instead of more work for teachers, the suggestion here is for a more honest recognition of the work teachers are already doing. Teachers all contribute to the creation of place in one way or another and progress toward intentionality in that role requires first admitting that it exists in the first place.

As discussed in this book, people shape place and give it meaning. Whether through physical changes to place, more inclusion of voices in understanding of place, or just interpretation of surroundings, humans are the essential actors in the creation of place. Teachers, through their work, will provide the setting in which the values and perspectives which will shape how students interact with place are developed. Teachers shape people, and people are the place.

Through their work in shaping future generations, teachers impact the creation of place. Although a bit indirect, communities and landscapes are the outcome of teachers' work. The service teachers provide students and their families may be generally recognized, but their service extends beyond students to communities and landscapes themselves. Teachers do not just exist in place, they are stewards of place.

SKILLSETS OF STEWARDS OF PLACE

In recognizing the role of teachers as stewards of place there is an opportunity to consider the skillsets which allow teachers to be successful in this role. Again, this is not a new role for teachers, but just a recognition of a role they already have. By extension, the skillsets necessary to serve as a teacher steward are not new, but are skills which already contribute to impactful teaching. However, the concern is that these skillsets are not often recognized or appreciate in evaluating teachers.

By and large most teacher evaluation centers around standardized assessment scores.[1] The skills which allow a teacher to prepare students to do well on assessments do not necessarily translate to that same teacher being able to serve as a steward of their community. In fact, aiming toward standardized assessments in many ways require teachers to ignore the needs of the local community to focus on the needs of the assessment.

Instead of skills focused on preparing students for an assessment, the skillsets of teacher which are effective stewards of place likely more closely mirror concepts of Nel Noddings's care theory.[2] Noddings proposed the concepts of modeling, dialogue, practice, and confirmation. Teachers who are able to be stewards of place are those which can apply these concepts to their communities. In short, teachers must care for their communities.

Teachers who care for their communities are those who model an ability to care, engage in dialogue with their communities, practice in care-giving activities for their community, and confirm the community's motives and actions. However, these concepts of care theory require the establishment of a relationship between the cared-for and care-er: in this case, the teacher and community.[3]

The ability to establish a relationship with the community, however, broadly defined is an essential skill for teachers as stewards of place. This is a skill which does not translate easily into standardized evaluation, as it is by definition context-specific. However, it is a skill which does translate into impactful practice. Recognizing teachers as stewards of place suggests that instead of evaluating teachers for whether they would be effective anywhere, administrators and policymakers should evaluate them for if they are impactful exactly where they are.

The place-specific work of teachers is indicative that teachers not only forms gestalts with place as humans, but they also do so in their craft. Some teachers do not just happen to be impactful where they are. Rather, they are great educators *because* of where they are. Teachers help create the place, but the inverse is also true in that the place helps create the teacher. In an era of increasing teacher shortages which are reaching a crisis point, this is a critical realization.

Many varied and diverse efforts are currently underway to help recruit and retain teachers to meet the needs of schools across the country. However, these efforts tend to focus on teachers in a few limited terms. First, they focus on if a school has enough teachers and if they are licensed. If there is an effort to consider beyond the first two criteria at all it tends to be limited to some very general definition of effectiveness.

However, as stewards of place, schools and communities do not just need a teacher, they need *their* teacher. Schools need teachers who care for communities and who are committed to creation of place in a way that allows the community to have long-term health and sustainability. Efforts to retain these teachers should not stop at considering the cost of finding a replacement teacher, but instead the lost value to the community to lose a steward.

Recognizing teachers as stewards of place also has implications for combatting the prevalent attempts to de-professionalize educators. Especially in the wake of school closures as a result of Covid-19 pandemic, there are growing narratives about the work of teachers not being overly specialized or difficult. These narratives have been aided in many states by the relaxing of standards to become a teacher. The stream of oxygen fueling the flame of these narratives is the perception that, whether because of their time as students or their role as parents, most adults understand the scope of what teachers do.

However, recognizing teachers as stewards of place provides a direct challenge to these narratives. Teachers are not just the people who help a student learn to sound out words. Their work quite literally helps determine the future of communities and landscapes. Cobbling together an argument to not fairly compensate an individual who helps a child learn phonics is its own uphill battle, but doing so for the people who will determine what a community is in the future seems downright asinine. In this light, undercompensating teachers is analogous to hiring a discount plastic surgeon, but for an entire community.

THE COMPOSITION

The role of steward of place could feel a bit heavy for teachers, especially at a time when many are already fatigued. However, this heaviness can be relieved in seeing this role not just as a responsibility, but as an opportunity. Henri Lefebvre referred to place as an *oeuvre*, an artwork in which all members participate.[4] The reality is that although all members of a community should get to contribute to this creation, teachers have a particularly influential role.

The artistry of teachers is typically underappreciated, but very much exists.[5] Among the ways this artistry can be expressed is in places themselves. Communities and landscapes are impacted by the decisions teachers make. In so doing, teachers can embed their perspectives, experiences, and impressions in communities as a form of artistic expression. Teachers are artists and at least one of the canvases upon which their work can be created and displayed are communities themselves.

CONCLUSION

Although the work of teaching for place has always been important, the need is ever growing. Communities and landscapes face numerous threats including climate change, gentrification, environmental degradation, urban sprawl, pollution, and countless others. Maintaining the status quo is not an option. Places in their current form will not continue into the future. Although places have never existed in a single form in perpetuity, the current conglomeration of threats suggests that without intervention, future iterations will be less than pleasant.

With no choice to opt out of engaging with place, the important question educators must ask themselves is whether they are going to acknowledge their role in the creation of place or attempt to continue in willful naivety. The reality is that all teachers do and will teach about place. Each educator must choose if they will teach about place intentionally or haphazardly. Stated differently, teachers must choose if they will pick up the brush to put purposeful strokes on the canvas of place.

REFLECTION QUESTIONS

1. How does viewing yourself as a steward of place change your perception of your work as a teacher?
2. In what ways have the places where you live and teach helped shape you as an educator?
3. What actionable steps can you take in your practice as an educator to embrace your role as a steward of place?

NOTES

1. Derek Gottlieb, *Education Reform and the Concept of Good Teaching* (New York: Routledge, 2015).

2. Nel Noddings, *Educating Moral People* (New York: Teachers College Press, 2002).

3. Noddings, *Educating Moral People*.

4. Henri Lefebvre, *The Production of Space*, trans. Donald Nicholson-Smith (Malden, MA: Blackwell, 2009).

5. Emily Christine Bretl, *Shifting Sands: The Art of Ecological Place-Based Education* (ProQuest Dissertations Publishing, 2020).

About the Author

Dr. **Matthew Clay** is an assistant professor of Teacher Education at Fort Hays State University. He is a former secondary science teacher from rural Kansas, and his research focuses on the connections between education and place. He primarily teaches science teaching methods courses in his current position and enjoys exploring curricular, pedagogical, and technological innovations to better equip his pre-service teachers to create meaningful interactions with place for their students. He lives in Dighton, Kansas, with his wife and sons.

www.ingramcontent.com/pod-product-compliance
Lightning Source LLC
Chambersburg PA
CBHW020708270326
41928CB00005B/318

9 781475 873214